Criminal Justice and the Policy Process

Second Edition

James G. Houston
Phillip B. Bridgmon
William W. Parsons

UNIVERSITY PRESS OF AMERICA,® INC.
Lanham • Boulder • New York • Toronto • Plymouth, UK

Copyright © 2008 by
University Press of America,® Inc.
4501 Forbes Boulevard
Suite 200
Lanham, Maryland 20706
UPA Acquisitions Department (301) 459-3366

Estover Road
Plymouth PL6 7PY
United Kingdom

Library of Congress Control Number: 2008926479
ISBN-13: 978-0-7618-4034-3 (paperback : alk. paper)
ISBN-10: 0-7618-4034-6 (paperback : alk. paper)
eISBN-13: 978-0-7618-4177-7
eISBN-10: 0-7618-4177-6

∞™ The paper used in this publication meets the minimum
requirements of American National Standard for Information
Sciences—Permanence of Paper for Printed Library Materials,
ANSI Z39.48—1984

Contents

Preface

Criminal justice is a growing discipline that owes much of its identity to more established disciplines such as political science, economics, philosophy, sociology, and psychology. Our approach in this text is to draw upon these disciplines in order to depict the complex nature of public policy analysis. There are many good texts on crime, justice, public policy, and policy analysis, but none synthesize the leading models of policy development into a coherent framework for understanding how crime policy is developed. Further, the administration of justice is an extension of policy making. Thus, we dedicate a significant portion of this text to the policy implications of justice administration. It is through policy implementation that choices are made among competing courses of action that ultimately determine government action.

Our goals for this text is to provide students of public policy with an understanding of the policy process and an appreciation for justice administration. Too often, public servants are left to carry out policies that are not rooted in empirical causes while simultaneously tending to the political environment that characterizes their work. Thus, we hope to also impart an appreciation for politics in both policy and administration. Once students appreciate that politics is not entirely undesirable, but should be expected and welcomed in many regards, the road to being a successful citizen, public servant, and colleague is more manageable.

Chapter One

Overview of Public Policy Analysis

LEARNING OBJECTIVES

In this chapter, you will do the following things:

1. Learn what is meant by policy and demonstrate how the concept of policy differs from rules, regulations, or procedures
2. Develop a working definition of policy analysis and discover the goal of policy analysis
3. Explore why criminal justice and corrections students and practitioners need to become familiar with the basic tools of policy analysis
4. Be introduced to a basic framework for analysis that is developed and thoroughly examined throughout the text
5. Be able to identify the five basic goals and objectives of this text and learn how the text is organized to assist you in achieving these goals and objectives.

> Sometimes politics gets in the way of good policy
>
> —Arlan Specter, U.S. Senator

WHY POLICY ANALYSIS IN THE FIELD OF CRIMINAL JUSTICE?

In a representative republic like the United States, government always chooses solutions to public problems from many competing proposals. How to best address the issue of crime and punishments is a policy area similar in most respects to other policy problems. In some profound ways, however, justice policies are more important than other policy areas in terms of their influence upon the lives of all citizens, the costs to our public treasury, and contribution to the public good. As such, justice policy is public policy and normatively is supposed to serve the public. Yet, everywhere we see discrepancies between our rhetoric on crime and punishment and the choices government makes regarding this public problem. For example, we use get tough on crime rhetoric, but sentencing differences between street and white collar crime are very stark. The central purpose of this text is describing how this disconnect between our words and our deeds happens easily in regards to crime policy and without a sense of urgency in closing the gap.

To illustrate our approach to understanding public policy, we choose one aspect of the justice system. For us the passage of the USA Patriot Act provides an ideal policy area to demonstrate the choices we've made regarding how best to protect society from harm. Further, the complexity of policy problems and how to correct them are more than adequately demonstrated by focusing on terrorism and our policy responses to it. Ultimately, policies such as the Patriot Act are salient to average citizens and practitioners alike. Everyone has an opinion on crime and punishment with most being ready to share their views. Due to this, the policy process tends to cater to the public's attentiveness and understanding of punishment.

Many useful texts describe various theoretical models to understand policy. We add incrementally to these understanding by borrowing and adapting many of these perspectives. The shortcomings presently in the literature are that only a handful of texts deal with the justice policy process from a theoretical perspective. We seek to fill the void by developing a model of policymaking, applying it to the USA Patriot Act, and discussing the implications for practioners. Knowing how government arrives and decisions, implements them, and evaluates those endeavors is a necessary requisite for adequate citizenship.

POLICY DEFINED

Thomas Dye defines policy as what government chooses to do (Dye, 2002). Yet, criminal justice policy is much more. For example, we have a policy on maintaining prisons and a policy on providing adequate protection for the public by the police. All of those policies must be put into operation, and it is up to the criminal justice practitioner to put public policy into operation. Thus, policy differs from the administration or implementation of the policymaking process, but it is just as important for understanding how government goes about its work. Administration is simply an extension of policymaking.

In our view, a policy may be defined as general philosophical principles that guide the development of specific programs designed to address concerns associated with a broad issue. Certo defines policy as "a standing plan that furnishes broad, general guidelines for channeling management thinking toward actions consistent with reaching organizational objectives" (Certo, 1985). Jones identifies a number of policy "ingredients" including goals, plans, programs, decisions, and effects (Jones, 1984). Pressman and Wildavsky point out that policies "contain both goals and the means for achieving them" (Pressman and Wildavsky, 1973).

Criminal justice issues are greatly influenced by public opinion, special interests, the political whims of elected officials, constitutional restrictions, and the resources dedicated to solving them. These are just a few of the many forces that influence the world of the criminal justice practitioner. Yet, either for expediency or perhaps out of frustration, criminal justice students and practitioners often find that implementation is the primary measure of policy performance.

For example, a police chief will state that the department has a policy on traffic control, or a prison warden will state that a policy exists regarding family visitation of inmates. The use of the term *policy* to describe these activities is often inappropriate. Traffic control and visitation privileges are examples of activities performed by law enforcement or correctional agencies, but in and of themselves ought not to be thought of as policies. These examples more likely reflect the bureaucrat's desire to expedite paperwork and neatly fit people, places, and objects into pigeonholes. The routine can and does influence policy, but it is not the only factor contributing to policy performance.

The bureaucrat may feel isolated behind the mounds of paperwork, but his or her activities are greatly affected by others. Criminal justice policies, as with all issues, are the product of multiple influences and are of interest to a multitude of disciplines. Procedures are steps that must be followed when issues arise during the day-to-day work of justice professionals. Keeping policy analysis separate from administration is an important step in understanding the influences on the work of justice professionals.

These efforts to define policy commonly view the importance of developing well-thought-out plans and ultimately the importance of measuring the performance of those plans. Policy, therefore, is broader and more complex than simply recording visits to prisoners or issuing traffic citations. Rules and regulations are only one piece of the puzzle. It is the function of the policy analyst to define the number of pieces and to put the pieces of the puzzle together to develop a clearer picture of what the problem is, what can and should be done about the problem, and whether the policy addresses the problem.

_ GOTO Pg 13

For criminal justice students and practitioners, some of the major pieces of the policy puzzle include developing an understanding of politics, the political process, bureaucracy, constitutional law, and public management as well as expertise in corrections, law enforcement, and behavioral issues. Meaningful participation in crime policy requires an outward-looking approach to one's professional life, not isolation or a comfort zone associated with the routine and mundane aspects of daily operations.

THE INTERDISCIPLINARY NATURE OF POLICY ANALYSIS

Today, policy analysis is increasingly interdisciplinary. As problems and issues become more complex, scholars and researchers increasingly call on multiple disciplines to increase their information base and search for alternative causes, effects, and influences on policy. Issues today involve science, technology, and statistics as well as politics and social conditions. It is impossible for a single individual to become an expert in every field and explain everything that is wrong in the world simply by coming into contact with all that there is to study and observe.

Yet, the complex world in which we live tempts scholars not only to become aware of other disciplines but also, at a minimum, to be novice students of other fields of inquiry. The universe of possible points of study is narrowed by a particular issue or problem that interests the individual. For instance, there are economists interested in finding market solutions for environmental issues that traditionally would seem to be the purview of biologists and chemists. There are psychologists who become involved in the realm of medical recovery realizing that the success of therapy and rehabilitation can be psychological as well as physiological. And there are political scientists who study issues such as crime to gain a better understanding of the political process and the effects of that process on crime policy.

To better understand and make recommendations on how to improve policy, the field of political science increasingly crosses over into many other disciplines. For example, today's political scientists are experts in political sociology and political economy. Others have combined knowledge of government and politics with statistics and research methods. Still others are students of public policy who tend to focus on a particular issue and, by necessity, develop at least a minimum understanding of legal, technical, and scientific aspects of problems such as the environment, healthcare, and crime.

Some of these political science policy experts work within government itself and seek to improve policy from within the system. Many, however, are scholars and researchers in private and public universities and research organizations. Regardless of their locale, the field of political science today is effecting change in specific issues. For political scientists to function effectively in analyzing particular issues, they become at a minimum amateur experts in the field of inquiry.

In the field of criminal justice, for example, the political scientist ought to have a basic understanding of corrections, police management, and causes of crime, to name a few. James Q. Wilson's *Thinking about Crime* (1983) is an excellent example of political science inquiry into the field of crime policy grounded in clear scholarly thinking. Unfortunately, few studies of this nature and sophistication are generated among criminal justice scholars.

POLICY DISCUSSION IN CRIMINAL JUSTICE LITERATURE

The discipline of criminal justice is an ideal setting for incorporating policy analysis as an effective means for addressing crime issues. The day-to-day activities of the criminal justice practitioner produce a certain degree of expertise. Further, students of criminal justice need to become familiar with the methods employed by other disciplines to observe and analyze crime policy. After all, if outsiders are going to take the time to learn the basics of corrections and police management, then it should go without saying that criminal justice students and practitioners should develop an understanding of the practices and methods of other disciplines that study the crime issue.

As noted earlier, Wilson's *Thinking about Crime* (1983), originally published in 1975, offers students of criminal justice a political science perspective toward crime. Wilson's emphasis is on the politics and issues important to the formulation of crime policy. Wilson claims to be distraught over the liberal and conservative debate toward the crime issue that continuously polarizes American political elites. Wilson states that liberals in the 1960s and early 1970s denied that crime was increasing and instead contended that "crime in the streets was a rhetorical cover for racist sentiments." If crime was increasing, according to the liberal position, it was doing so because government was failing to invest enough money in federal programs aimed at unemployment and poverty, all of which could contribute to the prevention of crime and could further foster rehabilitation of offenders in the community rather than in prisons.

Conservatives, on the other hand, asserted that crime was destroying America and that the only way to fight it was to "support your local police," impeach Chief Justice Earl Warren, and reverse the Supreme Court rules that were 'handcuffing' the police, appoint a 'get tough' attorney general, and revive the death penalty." Both of these approaches were and continue to be off the mark, according to Wilson. *Thinking about Crime* was intended mainly as an informative tool to challenge decision makers to think more substantively and less ideologically about crime issues.

In this regard, the Wilson text is probably the leading text in the effort to rethink approaches toward crime. Yet, it is not instructive in how to engage in policy analysis or assist criminal justice practitioners and scholars in ways to improve criminal justice policy. Wilson offers little insight towards how to produce and implement a more effective crime policy. Probably the other noteworthy crime policy discussion is Samuel Walker's *Sense and Nonsense about Crime and Drugs* (1994).

This text also examines liberal and conservative attempts to deal with the social issues of crime and drugs. Walker asserts that neither approach has worked because both rely on theological views of society that are based not upon evidence but rather on certain canons that are not alterable by facts. Conservatives argue that "we can reduce crime if we just get tough with criminals. . . . Crime flourishes because the criminal justice system fails to arrest, prosecute, and punish dangerous offenders." If conservatives view the world as a large family where discipline and self-control should rule, liberals view the world as a large classroom where the less fortunate people can learn ways to overcome their adversity. Liberals argue that people "do wrong because of bad influences in the family, the peer group, or the neighborhood, or because of broader social factors, such as discrimination or the lack of economic opportunity."

Walker leads the reader through the criminal justice system, liberal and conservative crime control philosophies, and the current emphasis on drugs—the hysteria surrounding drugs, their impact, and control strategies. *Sense and Nonsense about Crime and Drugs* is an excellent book and no doubt has enlightened and challenged the thinking of many people about crime. However, its shortcoming is that while it informs, it fails to instruct the reader on how to educate a shortsighted public and myopic public officials, or how to implement a more effective approach to fighting crime. In fact, as Walker points out, nothing works—neither the liberal nor the conservative approaches to dealing with crime. Readers are left with a feeling of helplessness when they should be able to grab a tool or tools to begin the job of making things work.

Criminal justice students are challenged to communicate effectively with scholars, officials, and experts from other disciplines interested in the crime issue. Optimistically, effective dialog with others familiar with crime issues ought to occur for the sake of knowledge and a sincere commitment to the betterment of policy. If we recognize that some political scientists may find value in learning the particulars of the field of criminal justice, then we ought to consider the utility of criminal justice students becoming familiar with the

problems in society and government were a genuine adherence to the principles of policy analysis, then most, if not all, of our worldly problems would
be solved already. Policy analysis is not a panacea for solving problems. It is
a scientific method for understanding and increasing the chances of improving policy. Further, any policy analysis is only as sound as the competency of
the individuals conducting the research on a given problem or issue.

In a somewhat sarcastic contrast, Wildavsky (1979) offers a less optimistic
view of our ability to define, let alone conduct, policy analysis when he points
out, "Policy analysis serves organizations of people who want to correct their
mistakes." While Mood and others imply perfection and problem solving,
Wildavsky emphasizes error correction, and, in our view, rightfully so. Those
who seek to analyze policy for the sole purpose of solving problems are
doomed to produce one failed policy after another. Neither government, nor
humanity, in general, is perfected to the point where problem solving is a certain outcome of policy analysis. In contrast, human beings are quite adept at
creating problems. Thus, the goal of policy analysis is to expose problems and
errors created by people and to offer insight on how we might correct past
mistakes, knowing full well that attempts to improve policy are likely to be
error-laden and equally deserving of close scrutiny.

While some scholars may be more optimistic than others with respect to
the prospects and limitations of policy analysis, there is general agreement
that an effective policy analysis is comprehensive and recognizes the multiple causes and effects associated with government activity. However, per-
forming what is tantamount to scientific research in a political setting raises
some interesting dilemmas for the researcher. On the one hand, recognizing
that "everything explains everything" tends to make research too cumbersome and potentially irrelevant. On the other hand, too narrow a focus, where
the researcher seeks to determine the single most important cause of a problem, can fail to take into account the complex nature of political and social issues. A narrow focus based on incomplete or wrong assumptions about an issue also may produce highly irrelevant results.

Understanding macro-level politics and government is also a critical starting point. Appropriate research methods materialize once a general understanding of issues and politics occurs. Thus, this text is organized along a
three-step progression. First, we examine criminal justice policy from the
macro level and provide a basic public policy framework or model for re-
searching and developing a basic understanding of national and state crime
policies. Second, we apply the framework and provide an overview of the
crime issue and criminal justice policy today. Third, we discuss tools and
techniques for analyzing criminal justice policies as they are carried out by
the practitioner at the micro level.

Interest in policy analysis at both the macro and micro levels of government has produced many theories, frameworks, and models for the study of politics and issues. We will review many of these approaches to policy analysis throughout the text. Some of these approaches include systems theory, behavioralism, rational-actor theory, incremental theory, and communications theory. However, in an introductory text such as this, it is our intent to discuss only the basics of these models, revealing some of the advantages and disadvantages of these techniques of inquiry. As students become more practiced at policy analysis, their interests and needs will move them more extensively towards mastering one or more of the methods of analysis introduced in this text. A great deal of guidance towards mastery of these techniques can be found in the suggested readings in the bibliography at the end of this book.

This text is designed to provide a basic framework for conducting a policy analysis that will produce satisfactory and meaningful results, even for the novice researcher. According to Charles O. Jones (1984), an effective framework for analysis "should enable you to unravel how the policy process works in the United States" regardless of the issue under study. Keeping with this theme, our framework for analysis incorporates the insights of Jones' *An Introduction to the Study of Public Policy* (1984), Anderson's *Public Policymaking: An Introduction* (1997), Dahl's classic text *Who Governs* (1961), Lindblom and Woodhouse's *The Policy-Making Process* (1993), and Easton's *A Systems Analysis of Political Life* (1979).

The insights of these scholars emphasize the forces that influence: (1) how a problem gains the attention of government; (2) how the problem is influenced by politics; (3) what government does; and (4) whether government handles the problem effectively. This simple four-step approach serves as the foundation for our analysis of criminal justice policy. It is also our goal, and sincere belief, that once this four-step technique of inquiry is mastered, the criminal justice student has an adequate grounding to produce a basic yet meaningful policy analysis of any criminal justice issue.

A FRAMEWORK FOR ANALYSIS

The model we apply to better understand criminal justice policy more commonly would be recognized as a variation of the public policy cycle and is extensively developed in Chapter 3. For now, let us briefly examine some of the scholarly thinking relating to the policy process. The number of steps involved varies from one scholar to another. Jones (1984), for example, identifies no less than fifteen "initial realities" of government, which leads him to a five-step approach to understanding the policy process: policy formulation, legitimation, appropriation, implementation, and evaluation. Anderson (1997) also develops his model around five concepts that vary slightly in terminology from Jones but follow pretty much the same steps: policy agenda, policy formulation, policy adoption, policy implementation, and policy evaluation. These scholars help define the playing field and game rules on which policy rests, but policy is more than a beginning and an ending process. A complete analytical framework of public policy needs to recognize the cyclical or systemic nature of what government does.

Easton's systems theory is based on the simple notion that politics easily can be examined as the relationship between inputs and outputs. Viewed as a system, however, Easton (1979) asserts that politics cannot simply be studied as a beginning and ending process. A complete political system encompasses integrated realities, coherence, endurance, and interdependence in a complex setting (Susser 1992). Thus, perhaps a major contribution of systems theory is that policy and politics are circular. Feedback in both analytical and political forms exposes errors in previous policies and promotes the continuation of the policy process. In essence, the policy process becomes cyclical in nature. Viewed in this perspective, systems theory helps better define what government does and why. Systems theory also is better at explaining the development of policy over time. Feedback gained from a systems analysis of American public policy confirms the incremental nature of the policy process as illustrated by Charles Lindblom (1959) in his classic article, "The Science of Muddling Through."

While Jones and Anderson recognize and confirm the systemic nature of policy, this is not the thrust of their discussions. Jones and Anderson are primarily interested in examining what happens at each step of the process and where each step can be improved. They imply that by perfecting the policy process, policy will improve over time. In a similar vein, systems analysis recognizes the importance of feedback (Easton, 1979). Review of past as well as current decisions is necessary to make informed judgments and positive adjustments to future policies.

Originally, Lindblom (1959) asserted that all policy is incremental, which fits well into our developing framework. However, in a later work (Lindblom and Woodhouse, 1993), Lindblom wrestles with the fact that some policies are quickly formulated and implemented while others move incrementally. Nevertheless, Lindblom sees politics as the product of past decisions, trial, and error. Decisions for the most part are necessarily based on previous policies since the future is unforeseen. Fearful of change, decision makers make incremental adjustments based on what worked or failed to work in the past.

Thus, error correction becomes the primary benefit of policy analysis. Policy analysis is unlikely to succeed at spontaneous problem solving, and more likely to produce policy succession (Wildavsky, 1979).

Ultimately, the task of the policy analyst is to develop and implement a framework for analyzing what has occurred; and as objectively as possible, to fashion alternatives for a succeeding and improved policy over its predecessor. The model in this text allows the beginning criminal justice policy analyst to observe the past and the present political arena; based on these observations, the student is exposed to strategies and tools for making policy recommendations.

The basic model assists the student in identifying the inputs affecting criminal justice policy, observing government operations influencing policy, and evaluating the strengths and weaknesses of current crime policies, and it challenges the student to produce feedback to decision makers and make recommendations for improving American criminal justice policy. Chapter 3 examines each policy step in greater detail. For each step, the researcher can apply specific strategies and tools to ascertain what is happening to any issue at each step of the policy cycle.

The first three steps are all important if the analysis of the policy is to produce meaningful feedback for researchers, and more importantly for decision makers. For example, during the input stage we will explore several theories of communication and participation as explanations of the agenda-setting process. We will explore government operations to examine influence factors such as the legislative process, ideology, and incrementalism on current crime policies. During our examination of outputs, or what government produces, we will discuss the nuances of implementation relations as influences on crime policy. Finally, during our discussion of feedback, and particularly in Part Three of the text, "Policy Analysis and the Practitioner," we will examine the many tools available to the policy analyst for evaluating policy and for making sound policy recommendations. Some of these tools include developing mission statements, agency strategic planning, and management by objectives, and factor evaluation. A key ingredient to our approach is the concerted effort that is made to incorporate a real policy into the framework. While there are many texts on public policy and policy analysis, most simply offer the theory and tools.

Few take the opportunity to apply scientific frameworks to actual policies, choosing instead to allow the individual researcher to adapt the abstract to the real world. Our hope is to bring policy to life by offering our own variation of tried-and-tested analytical techniques to the contemporary criminal justice policy arena. By taking a walk through a basic analysis of today's crime policy, we seek to increase the comfort level of the criminal justice student and practitioner in conducting policy analysis. Once familiar with the basics of policy analysis, the student and/or practitioner then may apply the same processes to more specific problems within the broad spectrum of what constitutes crime policy.

The student and practitioner also are challenged to more extensively fine-tune their analytical skills than is possible through an introductory text. In a sense, the entire book is a framework for analysis, but it is only a beginning, and we learn by doing. For criminal justice policy to improve even incrementally, researchers and practitioners must do more than simply read a text on policy analysis. They must make a serious commitment to expanding their library of knowledge in the field. Scholars, students, and practitioners in the field of criminal justice need to be asking the tough questions and seeking the tough answers, rather than simply sitting back and evaluating policy performance on whim, impression, or rhetoric.

INCORPORATING POLICY ANALYSIS INTO THE FIELD OF CRIMINAL JUSTICE

The actions of criminal justice officials are influenced both directly and indirectly by external forces. Many of these forces are subtle and not easily recognized unless a concerted effort is made to embrace policy analysis as a vital component of an organization's activities. Crime policy is historically quite often a symbolic issue for elected officials. Campaign rhetoric abounds in the area of getting tough on crime. We need look no further than the presidency to observe the reliance on symbols over substance when dealing with the crime issue. The Reagan years produced Nancy Reagan's "Just Say No" campaign. The Senior Bush administration declared a "War on Drugs" that amounted to little more than a skirmish on cocaine. During President Clinton's administration, crime legislation put more police officers on the streets and banned "cop killer guns." Presidential crime initiatives are typically "feel good" measures that offer little substantive hope of addressing the root causes of crime and thus permanently reducing crime. Neither the Clinton administration nor the Republican's who have controlled Congress over the past decade, to date, have offered a substantive alternative policy towards crime in the United States. Instead, the tried-and-tested political rhetoric—so effective in short-term campaigning—dominates the crime debate (Gimpel, 1996).

Promoted as substantive policies, the symbolic treatment of crime issues presents real problems for criminal justice agencies and practitioners. Agencies are charged with carrying out the law, laws that for the most part are the product of legislative and executive action. If presidents, the Congress, governors, state legislators, and city governments produce laws that are simply politically popular without considering the likelihood of successful implementation, then law enforcement agencies are placed in the awkward position of being required to carry out directives that are flawed long before crossing the administrator's desk.

Surely it is in the best interest of the criminal justice official to distinguish errors made within the agency from those that are the product of external forces, which are seemingly out of the administrator's direct control, yet potentially influence the success or failure of policy. The criminal justice practitioner who reviews only operating procedures as the standard for policy analysis neglects the many other factors contributing to policy failure. Basic analytical skills are needed to distinguish substance from symbol, law from rhetoric, procedures from policy, and internal from external influences on policy.

Criminal justice students and practitioners constantly must search for errors, causes of the errors, and remedies for past mistakes. At a minimum, students are challenged to identify mistakes in policy, even if remedies do not readily present themselves. There is often little the criminal justice bureaucrat can do to change the political rhetoric associated with a hot issue such as crime. Symbolic policies and "feel good" measures may be an inevitable component of controversial issues. But the bureaucrat armed with the tools to conduct a comprehensive policy analysis is able to distinguish fact from myth and substance from rhetoric, and become better informed about the world in which he or she is expected to perform functions and duties. The student of criminal justice who understands and embraces policy analysis is better equipped to understand the forces behind the policy. The criminal justice practitioner who embraces policy analysis is better equipped to communicate with other practitioners, elected officials, scholars, and the various disciplines regarding the entirety and complexity of criminal justice issues.

GOALS AND OBJECTIVES OF CRIME POLICY ANALYSIS

The primary goal of policy analysis is to determine if a particular policy truly addresses the public problem it was created to solve. Analysis also includes an examination of the process by which policies are created. Policies and their success or failure cannot be separated from one another. As such, there are many questions worthy of exploration in public policy analysis. Some of the questions asked in this text are: What external political and societal forces are influencing the criminal justice practitioner's work and his or her agency's mission? Are the rules and procedures established and carried out by the agency integral to crime policy, or are they merely routine, day-to-day activities with little or no substantive impact on crime? Does the agency have adequate tools and resources to carry out its mission? If not, is the problem internal, one the agency can correct, or is the problem out of the agency's control, perhaps reflecting external political and social forces? Should criminal justice students, practitioners, and agencies become more aware of and participate more in the entirety of the policy process, or is it enough to implement rules, regulations, and procedures? What are the benefits and costs of a comprehensive analytical approach to criminal justice policy? What results realistically should be expected from a policy analysis?

In the search for answers to these questions, the text has several goals and objectives.

1. To acquaint the student with the primary theories and models guiding contemporary policy analysis
2. To develop a framework for the comprehensive analysis of criminal justice policy
3. To identify and explain the various influences on crime policy
4. To develop the basic skills of policy evaluation
5. To enable the student to make informed judgments on his or her role as a participant and analyst in the field of criminal justice
6. To instruct the student on how to develop organizational policies and procedures within the parameters of institutional guidelines

We attempt to assist the student in answering the questions we have raised and in achieving the goals and objectives of the text through a variety of techniques. First, each chapter begins with a case study that poses a problem relating to the chapter. Second, study-guide objectives assist the student in the retention of the key points of the chapter. Additionally, the learning objectives seek to challenge the reader to link the more theoretical nature of each chapter to the real world as presented in the case study. Third, review questions conclude each chapter to offer the student the opportunity to explore in more depth a topic or concept of particular interest.

All contemporary social, political, and economic issues demand objective and comprehensive analysis, as well as skilled practitioners conducting analytical studies. Our contention is that such studies are seriously lacking in the field of criminal justice and crime policy. In fact, criminal justice scholars have largely ignored the subject and the serious student is left to the field of political science for guidance in matters relating to public policy and policy analysis.

Further, the inattention to policy analysis in this area cannot help but create a void for the criminal justice practitioner or analyst who sincerely wants to perform his or her job effectively. In this text, we seek to assist the criminal justice student and practitioner in finding ways to bring crime policy to life. That is, if we are to be successful in improving crime policy, all those interested in this field of inquiry need to be armed with the tools, skills, and knowledge necessary for the effective formulation, implementation, and evaluation of policy as it relates to crime and its etiology.

OUTLINE OF THE TEXT

Beginning in Chapter Two, we provide a discussion of the influences and forms of participation effecting crime policy. A typology or framework on participation in politics and policy is developed to improve understanding of why and how policy advocates influence crime policy. The typology is intended to assist the student of public policy in identifying the motives and goals of policy advocates. A key aspect of Chapter Two is to reveal the tools of effective lobbying. We also explore the strategies and tactics of influential participation. Basically, we answer these questions: "Who are the most influential decision makers in crime policy? What strategies and tactics are influential in government policymaking and in particular crime issues? What are the motivations of policy advocates in the American political system, and in particular crime policy?

Chapter Three identifies the forces at work influencing and directing criminal justice policy during the input, government operations, implementation, and feedback stages of the policy cycle. The strategies and tactics of effective political participation developed in Chapter Two are incorporated into the policy process. Chapter Four builds on Chapter Three and draws conclusions as to the political realities influencing crime policy outcomes as practiced at the national level. Chapter Four also offers the opportunity to analyze up-to-date efforts to protect the United States from future terrorist attacks. We apply our framework to the tapestry that falls under the heading "corrections policy."

Chapter Five begins to offer insight on the development of mission statements, rules, and procedures that complement public policy. Ultimately, policies must be administered. Administration is simply an extension of policy making (Hupe and Hill, 2002). We emphasize establishing rules and procedures that contribute to the effective implementation of the overall policy, not rule-making simply for the sake of expediting paperwork.

Chapter Six provides an overview of the planning side of public policy. We discuss tactical and strategic planning along with basic tools for effective agency planning. This chapter explores the interconnectedness of the political process, planning, and methods for coping with the political realities associated with planning. Chapter Seven conveys the ever-increasing quantitative nature of public policy analysis and reviews statistical methods and quantitative tools. We explore strengths and weaknesses of quantitative research methods. The goal of applying scientific research methodology is to improve objectivity and increase rationality in policymaking. We examine the prospects and limitations of increasing objectivity in an otherwise subjective political setting.

Chapter Eight summarizes the text and offers concluding insights on improving the criminal justice policy through policy analysis. We review the public policy cycle (Chapter Four) and the participation typology (Chapter Three) for their utility as a technique for better understanding the criminal justice policy. The policy cycle reveals the many struggles, trials, and tribulations of policy development. Strategies and tactics for producing effective policies are explored. This chapter provides insights into the root causes of crime as well as the likelihood of developing and implementing a comprehensive set of crime reduction policies.

It is easy to view the crime issue as hopeless. In fact, much of our analysis reveals many pitfalls and shortcomings about crime policy. Nevertheless, we see a light at the end of the tunnel. As we discussed earlier in this chapter, policy analysis may be at its strongest when finding the errors of our ways. Having identified flaws, sound policy analysis also reveals alternative approaches in the effort to remedy past errors. Thus, we argue that policy analysis can play an important role in the criminal justice arena.

Policy analysis is not a panacea for problem solving. If attempted as such, any policy analysis is destined to fail and contribute to the criticism that extensive research is a waste of time, effort, and money. Policy analysis offers a scientific method for obtaining more and better information than is possible by relying simply on inference, anecdote, rhetoric, and politics. For this oversimplified reason alone, policy analysis is a meaningful and practical venture. Policy analysis is certainly an important activity to encourage in the field of criminal justice where factors such as popular perceptions and political game playing are readily apparent. Let the research begin.

SUMMARY

Public policy may be defined as a set of general philosophical principles that guide the development of specific programs designed to address concerns associated with a broad issue. It is a standing plan that furnishes broad, general guidelines for channeling management thinking towards actions consistent with reaching organizational objectives.

Policy analysis is increasingly interdisciplinary in nature. For criminal justice practitioners to be effective, they must have a basic knowledge of disciplines vital to effective policy research such as political science, corrections, police organization, and the law, to name a few. After all, criminal justice policy is the product of government and politics. No serious effort to address any issue, let alone crime, can take place without an understanding of and appreciation of how government and politics influence policy outcomes.

The purpose of this text, then, is to introduce students and practitioners to a framework for a comprehensive analysis of crime policy. Readers will examine inputs (how problems are brought to government), government operations (how decisions are made), outputs (how government action occurs), and feedback (how to evaluate policy). Only through a good understanding of the processes central to policy analysis can we begin to approach crime issues in a more objective and effective manner than is currently the case in a political environment wrapped up in a liberal versus conservative blame game.

REVIEW QUESTIONS

1. Define the following concepts:
   a. public policy
   b. policy analysis
   c. inputs
   d. government operations
   e. outputs
   f. feedback
2. Lindblom states that public policy is incremental. Wildavsky sees policy analysis as a means for error correction. Are these two perspectives compatible? Why or why not?
3. Distinguish between macro-level and micro-level decision making.

Chapter Two

Influences on Criminal Justice Policy

LEARNING OBJECTIVES

In this chapter, you will do the following:

1. Identify three ingredients needed to form an effective interest group
2. Discover how special interests are able to use these ingredients effectively in influencing crime policy
3. Learn the basic strategies available to political interests or policy advocates to influence policy generally, and crime policy specifically
4. Explore the tactics, political interests, or policy advocates use to influence the direction of policy generally, and crime policy, specifically
5. Describe elites, pluralists, ideologues, and rational "game players"

INTRODUCTION

Students of justice policy can rightly ask why, with all this data on crime, can't we come up with a *real* crime policy?" "Why does it seem that so many people have different sets of data and different solutions?" "Can't we at least come to an agreement on what the statistics are and what they mean?" Responding to these questions requires a deep understanding of the political and policy process. For it is not simply the level or quality (or lack thereof) of information that influences policy, but also and quite often more importantly, the most powerful political forces that guide policy outcomes.

This chapter examines macro-level policy decision making. The focus is on political influence and the flow of political power as it pertains to criminal justice issues. We explore who, what, where, why, and how information about crime influences national policy making. *Who* influences crime policy? *What* political strategies and tactics are the most effective means of influencing the crime debate? *How* is information about crime most likely to be used by decision makers?

WHO INFLUENCES CRIME POLICY?

Crime policy is primarily shaped according to the interests of moneyed elites. To be sure, the moneyed elite include the usual suspects of organized interests and citizens, but also include elite media, think-tanks, and business (Dye, 2002). Here, we focus on two primary shapers of crime policy: interest groups and the media.

Understanding how representation works is a key to answering the question of who influences crime policy. In a broad sense, representation is simply providing for a communications process between citizens and elected officials. A standard civics approach to this relationship might focus on elections, noting that citizens, through the ballot box, directly hold elected officials accountable by their vote. However, representation is far more complex than simply studying the electoral connection that exists between the voter and the candidate. In American politics, studies on representation include special interests, lobbying, government agencies, the media, public opinion, and political parties, to name a few.

Many scholars view no electoral forms of linkages as more important to understanding policy outcomes than the results of any single election. (*See*, for example, Dye, 1995 especially chapter 8; Schattschneider, 1975; and Bennett, 1996) Election results rarely produce a significant influence or impact on policy. Work on policy occurs after the election, and typically after the public has lost direct interest in the inner workings of government (Bennett, 1996).

Decision makers confront issues, including crime, every day. Most citizens, while genuinely concerned, make statements on issues only sporadically, typically only during elections; or by expressing their opinion through a public opinion poll, or occasionally venting their feelings to the media as a reaction to a crisis such as the Oklahoma City bombing. On a day-to-day basis, even if a dedicated official strives for the "public's" input, it cannot be found. Instead, the elected representative or senator is relegated to dealing with unelected, self-proclaimed representatives of the public interest such as interest groups and lobbyists.

One common complaint about government is its cozy ties with special interests. The public abhors insiders, lobbyists, and the ideologues who, in their view, are controlling the decisions of elected officials. The public consistently seeks ways to force these "vultures" out of government rather than rise up and participate en masse to counter such influence or perhaps to steer the direction of special interests. Term limits, campaign finance reform, lobbying restrictions, and the like are all ways of reducing the possibility of an elected official being unduly influenced by special interests and in theory allow the official to become more closely connected to the people.

The reality is that the public already has more than adequate means to contact officials other than by election. Members of Congress hold open forums in congressional districts; yet, typically only special interest group members attend. Members of Congress through franking privileges periodically contact each and every voter by mail. Most of the literature reaches the recycling bin of the average citizen but becomes ammunition for the typical lobbyist. Computer technology and the information highway allow millions of citizens to send megabytes of ideas through cyberspace directly to policymakers, the media, and special interests. Yet, the public views the government as elusive, secretive, and inaccessible. Further, the public perceives this closed system of government as something conjured up by lobbyists and their enslaved politicians to grab power at the expense of the average citizen who is powerless to do anything about it.

The existence of a select set of effective interests in government rests less with government rules and procedures (although admittedly a contributing factor) and more with the resources these groups have to offer decision makers that the average citizen can rarely match (Wright, 1996). These resources can be divided into three components: time, money, and expertise. How does one effectively and consistently get the attention of an elected official? Effective lobbyists make the time commitment, sets aside financial resources, and make sure that they are engaged in and informed about the topic. The lobbyists put themselves in a position to converse with that representative every single day of the legislative session (Wright, 1996).

How is this different from the average citizen? The average citizen is worried about a nine-to-five job, mortgage payments, and coaching his daughter's softball game after work. The average citizen's time, money, and expertise allocation have been fully utilized at work and at home, leaving few resources for meaningful, long-term, and informed involvement in government. Enter the special interest groups, lobbyists, and paid professional experts interested in issues such as crime.

Special interest groups operate at various levels of government in pursuit of policies for their membership, but whenever politically beneficial, in the name of the average citizen as well. From the interest group's perspective, the public's cries are heard in government. In fact, from the view of special interests, the public would have no voice at all if not for the well-intentioned efforts of lobbyists. Some of the better-known special interest groups in crime policy development include the National Rifle Association (NRA), the American Civil Liberties Union (ACLU), the National Association of Mayors, the International Association of Police Chiefs, and the American Correctional Association, and lately victims' rights groups.

What are the implications of special interests on crime policy? The average citizen perceives crime to be an issue but has little direct advice to offer decision makers as to what to do about it. In the absence of clear public direction regarding crime, special interests are quick to offer numerous and varied approaches to the issue that run the spectrum from prevention to punishment, liberal to conservative, and protecting the accused versus the victim.

These varied definitions of crime are reflected in the views of special interest groups, which run the political spectrum. For example, the NRA views crime in light of attempts to control gun ownership. Making it easy for criminals to get guns and difficult for law-abiding citizens to defend themselves has contributed, in the NRA's opinion, significantly to the crime problem (politics of gun control). In contrast, the American Civil Liberties Union sees the crime issue solely from the perspective of questions surrounding civil liberties. In the absence of an informed and unified public, the crime issue will continue to be defined by entities and groups driven primarily by ideology or a "cause," not the public interest or the political "middle." This point is vital to understanding the politics of the crime issue. Most special interests in this issue claim their views are in the public interest. But such remarks are more often than not simply a claim to reflect ideological beliefs, not factual evidence.

The absence of an informed public allows for ideological interests to dominate the crime issue and to define the issue on behalf of the public. When the public does become vocal, the demand for action typically comes in the form of "do something." In response, decision makers search for answers, but seldom do they find answers through contact with the general public. Many legislators no doubt have heard the crowd shout, "That is why we elected you, to find the answers that we do not have!" Still searching for information and guidance, legislators find that the only source of information all too often is the special interests.

One important source of information often underused by legislators is practitioners and scholars associated with the field of criminal justice. Years of government service at the local, state, and national level provide these individuals with hands-on experience and readily accessible data to forge criminal justice policy. The expertise in this area also can be found in academia, where scholars in criminal justice, criminology, political science, psychology, and sociology, to name a few, often research crime issues from the viewpoint of their respective disciplines. These individuals have an advantage in that they have made commitments in time and developing expertise. They should be consulted and are readily available for consultation. What they lack are the financial resources and political prowess common to the most effective special interest groups.

Whether a special interest group such as the NRA or a professional bureaucratic organization such as the nation's police chiefs, there are many opportunities to become an advocate of crime policy proposals. The key to successful policy advocacy is twofold. First, the interested party needs to identify and participate in the group or organization that most closely reflects his or her viewpoints. Second, the individual must be an effective policy advocate. An effective policy advocate learns and uses the strategies and tactics of political participation to achieve a desired political gain or policy output. In American politics, policy development is only partially a scientific and rational endeavor. More often than not, the successful policy emerges because of keen awareness of the strategies and tactics of politics.

Media

With the advances in information technology, the media has become an important nonelectoral linkage between crime policy and the electorate. In 1980, the percentage of all news stories without a public policy component was measured at approximately 36 percent. This, of course, means that 64 percent of all news stories were based on some important political issue. By the late 1990s that number had dropped to approximately 50 percent. News also has developed a more sensationalist tone over time. Over the same time period, the level of sensationalism in news stories grew from approximately 22 percent to almost 40 percent. The number of stories that had crime and disaster as their subject grew from approximately 8–13 percent (Shorenstein Center, 2005).

These figures indicate that news is not only focusing less on traditional policy areas, but news stories are also chosen more frequently for their emotional impact. News stories are also increasingly negative. A typical thirty-minute major network evening news broadcast undoubtedly will cover the major political events of the day, but of the approximate twenty-three minutes of news time in that half hour, we also have seen a rise in the "newsworthiness" of other traditionally nonpolitical events such as the O.J. Simpson trial, medical advancements, weather issues, and human interest stories.

Frequently, even traditional political news stories will be diluted with sensational or human-interest centered themes.

For instance, a story headlining the CBS evening news in fact may focus on a recent bombing, but will also likely include information about the personal impact of the tragedy. In lieu of a strategic or political analysis of the situation, it would not be unusual for that story's producer to arrange for a personal interview with the victim's family or neighbor reminiscing about the victim's hobbies, faith, personal qualities or unwavering patriotism.

Modern media are also charged with the responsibility of providing context and meaning. The process of information transmission is a core function, but secondarily they must put some perspective and meaning to the stories they disseminate. A random story on civil unrest may give the reader the basic facts of the event, but when put in the context of the cost of oil or the "war on terror" the story has more meaning. A similar story on the poor may not be immediately noteworthy, but cast in a light which blames governmental policy, it has new importance. It is within this subject area that theories of agenda-setting, priming and framing take on their importance. The way the media selects, produces, and presents information can have measurable political effects.

The media's primary problem is that it struggles with accusations of bias and with low levels of trust. It appears to be in somewhat of crisis, whereby Americans appear to doubt the ability of the media to be fair and accurate. There is not so much a concern that the media will purposefully substitute one date or name for another, but that they consistently fail to present facts in a manner that conveys the true meaning of the subject matter, as if they are "spinning" reality for some other purpose.

Many Americans believe this purpose is a liberal political agenda. It is a fact that most journalists possess liberal political views. In recent studies, evidence suggests that journalists, as a group, are more liberal than many of America's most liberal congressional districts. Additionally, some research has shown that there is a systematic liberal bias in the media. There have also been anecdotal accounts of liberal bias, most notably in Bernard Goldberg's book *Bias* (2002). Harder evidence aside, what is perhaps most worrisome is that the much of the American public generally *think* that media outlets are liberally biased. In this instance, thinking something is true is practically as good as that thing actually being true. As long as media consumers have that impression, media bias might as well exist.

Conversely, there has been research to suggest that the media actually exhibits characteristics that suggest a conservative tendency. This is more than a suggestion that Fox News or CNBC's Dennis Miller show has conservative tendencies. There is a case to be made that values and norms of broadcast media, in general, are surprisingly sympathetic to modern American conservatism and corporate America. While this case may not be as strong, there are many that certainly consider it troublesome.

Simply put, assessing media bias is tremendously difficult. The primary task of establishing what is unbiased to begin with may be an impossible goal. Obviously, a story on presidential scandal can be tremendously negative, but completely free of bias. Measurement issues are made more difficult by having *no clear point of reference*. Other issues further complicate matters.

The media does indeed play a special role in both influencing citizens and elected officials. Moral panics, mentioned earlier in this chapter, create a stir within the electorate and elected officials to act on behalf of protecting the public. These moral panics lead policies that are not rational responses to clearly defined public problems. In the 1980s crack became the moral panic that led to the incarceration of many minorities, particularly poor black males. The result was prison crowding and more societal resources directed at solving a problem unsolvable with traditional incarceration. In the 1990s gun violence gripped the middle class for the first time when several teenage boys killed classmates and teachers in at Columbine High School in Colorado. Politicians immediately began proposing new gun control laws and a crackdown on video game violence. However, neither of these was ever expected to solve the problem of gun crime or violence.

Thus, the media shapes the reality of citizens primarily. Secondarily, elected officials pay attention to the media to pick up cues concerning how other elites perceive and understand national events. The media's gate-keeping role does not necessarily tell us what to think, but it certainly allows the media to shape what we think about. Interest groups also use the media to stir mass opinion and communicate effectively with likeminded souls who then can help put pressure on the policy process.

THE POLITICAL STRATEGIES FOR POLICY SUCCESS

In recent years, the battleground of crime policy has been waged between the liberal left and the conservative right. Both agree that crime is a problem, but are separated by extreme differences over the causes and solutions to crime issues. As elected officials, politicians have an obligation to listen to the public. Yet, all too often, ideologues are the only policy advocates willing to take the time, spend the money, and develop an expertise (albeit narrow) to be heard in government.

In politics, there are two primary strategies through which to effect change. Policy advocates may choose to either solicit cooperation to facilitate action or encourage conflict to increase awareness about a problem. The strategies are designed to generate demand and need as well as awareness. Either strategy can accomplish this goal. The two basic strategies simply differ as to the means for best achieving results.

The two contrasting styles are seen in former House Republican whip Robert H. Michel (D-IL) and former Speaker of the House Newt Gingrich (R-GA). Michel relied on cooperation and had a reverence for traditional institutional processes. Gingrich, however, relied more on conflict to effect change (Johnson and Broder, 1996). In fact, Gingrich's supposed outrageous and erroneous remarks to the media seemed to work at galvanizing public interest in legislation. Thus, he produced the impetus to quickly pass legislation, albeit in a very unorthodox style. However, as the 1996 elections approached, Gingrich toned down his conflict mode in favor of a more conciliatory approach with the White House as the president and Congress looked for a legislative success to present to would-be voters as opposed to congressional gridlock.

If policy advocates seek cooperation, they assume a world where, through negotiation, other participants with similar interests are open to compromise about a wide range of ideas. Time is not crucial in this policy environment. Political interests are more inclined to be concerned about long-term policy, political, and power relationships. Obviously, cooperation-seekers are under some pressure to ultimately produce a policy in a reasonable period of time. Political participants risk being ineffective if they spend most of their resources looking for allies and accomplishing little, and cooperation works best when there are few interests involved. Too many players make it harder to get everyone to sit down and cooperate with one another (Wildavsky, 1979).

Conversely, political actors engage in conflict when they see the urgency of a problem. Conflict-oriented political beings display little patience or tolerance for divergent opinions about issues. For the political actor who uses conflict, there is no better time than the present to bring a problem to the forefront and force a decision. The pressure to do something is paramount and far preferable over cogitation. This is especially true in a crowded policy arena where there appear to be many interests with a variety of viewpoints. If a political actor senses little hope of getting a variety of participants to work together, conflict may be the only recourse if there is indeed a sense of urgency. In the conflict environment, political actors must then be confident that they have the necessary skills to eventually emerge victorious (Wildavsky, 1979).

Political scientist and economist Anthony Downs identifies an issue-attention cycle where only during the initial stages of the discovery of a problem, during the euphoria surrounding the public's heightened awareness, is it likely that enough pressure can be brought on decision makers to act quickly (Downs, 1972). In this context, conflict thrives as a political strategy in contrast to cooperation, which requires time for all interested parties to come on board. Before a policy can be implemented, the actors must agree on a course of action. If Downs is correct, by the time cooperation occurs the public may have lost interest in the problem.

Those with conflict-oriented interests have no qualms about the problems of conflict. They simply set sail and follow the leader either down the policy direction proposed by the actor using conflict or towards a policy that will emerge once the political debate is underway. Hoping cooperation will someday emerge is a waste of time, energy, and resources. The conflict strategy assumes that heated debate has a better chance of producing action than long, drawn-out discussions that attempt to please everyone. The conflict approach assumes there always will be someone who cannot be convinced.

The effects of cooperation and conflict strategies on crime policy are readily apparent. From a cooperation perspective, the Clinton crime bill sought to please everyone by proposing tougher sentencing to satisfy conservatives and increasing spending for prevention to satisfy the liberal contingent. The problem with applying this strategy to the crime issue is the dominant policy advocates have ideological differences that are so severe that attempts to please everyone are summarily rejected under the principle that compromise in any form produces a policy that neither side supports but both believe is ultimately doomed to fail, albeit for different reasons.

Yet, the crime bill passed. In the end, cooperation emerged not because of the substantive elements in the bill, but it emerged because of appeals for cooperation made by both Democrats and Republicans that failure to pass a crime bill would have severe political consequences to legislators in the next election. Republicans, in voicing bitter opposition up to the final vote, geared up to make the crime bill a major component of campaign efforts to oust the Democrats from forty years of power. In the end, the focal point for cooperation was the pressure to do something. Since the passage of the crime bill, both sides continue to express misgivings and disappointment. As the new majority, Republicans in Congress are likely to want to revisit the crime bill to put their own identity on the issue.

For the criminal justice practitioner, developing a cooperation strategy is an important step in understanding intergovernmental relations. In a federal system of government where the national, state, and local authorities have distinct jurisdictions yet often need to coordinate their activities to carry out their function, cooperation is essential. However, there are limits to intergovernmental cooperation. Where long-range goals and comprehensive planning are required, cooperation among levels of government is essential and indeed does occur. Additionally, cooperation between layers of government is enhanced when the hierarchy of authority is clear, the goals to be accomplished in the cooperative effort are clear, and support is evident at all levels of law enforcement.

The American federal system makes effective coordination a dicey proposition. Coordination suggests hierarchy, centralization, and chain of command. By this definition of cooperation, the role of the national government becomes primary. Thus, federal law enforcement agencies have justification for altering state and local authority on the grounds that such interference reduces waste, fraud, and abuse of police power.

Yet, this sort of coordinated activity is highly criticized today. Political rhetoric, especially from the far right, condemns the overbearing heavy hand of Washington as the reason for policy failures, and the crime issue is no exception. Washington rules and regulations tie the hands of local law enforcement. Liberal Supreme Court decisions protect the criminal and enslave police officers who are trapped by the *Miranda* warnings and excessive search warrant requirements.

Federalism presupposes some degree of decentralization, with certain powers located at the federal level while other responsibilities remain at the state and local level. Cooperation is not built into the American political system, and too much unanimity in government always has been viewed with skepticism (Dionne, 1991). Federalism thus assumes that there are some issues and problems that are clearly best handled at the local level, but specifically who has jurisdiction over what is a two-hundred-year-old debate.

The crime issue serves as a good example of the dilemma federalism poses for the development and implementation of a coherent crime policy. It is only at the local level that all national, state, and local law agencies can coordinate their activities. It is primarily at the local level where crime occurs, laws are enforced, and justice is served. Thus, in federalism, cooperation does not have to depend on a top-down hierarchy. In fact, one of the appeals of a federal system is that cooperation is best achieved when instigated at the local level. Yet, as authority and responsibility are divided, coordination becomes more difficult. If emphasis is only on local enforcement, the national crime picture is easily ignored. States vary as to their financial resources, extent of crime, and philosophy of attacking crime.

Realizing that crime must be dealt with at various points in government tends to strain intergovernmental relations. In national politics today, there is a great debate over whether there should be more or less government. The reality is that the real question is whether to place more hierarchy and control in Washington or to shift greater responsibility to states and localities. A great deal of the appeal of decentralization seems to flow from the notion that

Washington is too closely tied to special interests. However, the skillful political being, well versed in the strategies and tactics of politics, can just as easily switch gears and focus efforts at a state or local setting. Contradictory state laws and court challenges to federal law also further strain intergovernmental coordination of crime policy.

Conflict is the preferred course of action for the ideologue and for single issue-oriented interests. For those whose interests have been ignored, or who see their once-superior position threatened, conflict may be the only way of keeping the attention of other decision makers. If one feels backed into a corner, conflict may be the only viable option for remaining a relevant participant in the process. However, effective conflict strategies require a sustained effort that is quite costly in terms of time and resources. Thus, conflict strategies are usually short term, designed to achieve a very specific goal as quickly as possible. Long-term goals and staying power take a back seat to the promise that swift and favorable change is forthcoming (Wildavsky, 1979).

Episodes of conflict are also common in crime policy. Death penalty advocates at one end of the political spectrum and gun control groups at the other are illustrative of groups with a narrow vested interest in crime who spare no expense to pursue singular goals. The overall day-to-day realities of dealing with criminals, law enforcement, the courts, and so forth, are secondary to conflict strategists who assume that all will simply fall into place once their pet policy is passed into law. Conflict on its own has not proven to be an effective political strategy over the long haul. The extent to which conflict can produce policy change depends greatly on the tactics adopted to carry out the strategy. For that matter, the cooperation strategy is also very dependent on employing effective and appropriate tactics to increase the prospects of policy success.

THE POLITICAL TACTICS FOR POLICY SUCCESS

The success of either the cooperation or conflict strategy rests with the political actor's ability to bring about a favorable policy decision. Whereas strategy involves the large-scale planning and directing of an operation designed to influence policy, tactics are the methods and procedures for accomplishing policy change. Two tactics serve as primary techniques for closing a policy deal: consensus building and political coercion. Both tactics are feasible whether operating under the cooperation strategy or the conflict model. How the strategies and tactics are combined requires a keen understanding of the political environment.

The consensus model emphasizes bargaining and compromise as the key to policy change. In the U.S. form of representative democracy, policy initiatives cannot occur without a majority agreement between the House, Senate, elected officials, the president, and the Supreme Court at the national level; support of state officials; and backing by local governmental entities. The assumption is that if any of the various official government entities are not behind the plan, then it will fail. The tactics include facilitating interaction among interests, listening to all sides, negotiating, mediating disputes, and searching for common points of agreement among diverse interests. It goes without saying that this approach is very time consuming and requires commitment and patience. Consensus models break down as a means of producing "good" policy in a crisis situation where haste seems more important than reason (Wildavsky, 1979).

The alternative tactic is coercion. Policy advocates can attempt to forgo a deeper understanding of alternative viewpoints and instead seek to sway others to their viewpoint through coercion (Widavsky, 1979). Rhetoric and propaganda are common coercion tactics. Appeals to patriotism, freedom, and "the American way" are positive techniques to rally forces behind a single idea. Fear tactics seem even more prevalent today as a way of both muffling opposition and rallying potential allies.

One of the most effective negative techniques today is to employ the "L" (liberal) word to stir up feelings of failure, frustration, and fear about big government. Concurrently, a greater degree of "moral" comfort can be gained by joining the conservative camp. Conservatives claim to hold the higher moral ground, stressing individual responsibility, family values, and "appropriate" lifestyles. The average citizen finds it difficult to raise objections to these concepts.

These tactics are central to understanding the crime policy game. Liberal views emphasize prevention; crime would vanish if we simply identified "at risk" individuals and improved their environment. An alternative view is to remove such individuals from an unhealthy environment and employ government to provide a therapeutic environment or programs such as midnight basketball to prevent crime. The average citizen is receptive to prevention rhetoric and few would argue against the rationale that we would be better off if we simply could prevent crime from happening.

Nevertheless, conservatives have done a masterful job of pointing out that liberal policies have been the predominant crime control strategy for at least thirty years and that prevention has failed miserably as a crime control policy. The conservative alternative is to use government as a behavioral role model rather than as an apologist for flaws in society. With respect to family values, conservatives agree that government ought to at least refrain from promoting unacceptable lifestyles (Wilcox, 1995).

Another conservative tactic is to emphasize the victim associated with crime. Victims must be protected, which means that the guilty must be punished swiftly and severely (Gimpel, 1996). Of course, this assumes that there is no such thing as a victimless crime and that all criminals are prosecuted. But the basic point put forth by conservatives is as equally difficult for the public to disagree with as that of the prevention-minded liberal. Very few Americans would openly oppose the prosecution and swift punishment of criminals. Few fail to have sympathy for a victim, more likely seeing themselves in that role than that of the accused. Combined with the growing concern over crime and the fact that the public feels it has thirty years of evidence that prior policies have failed, there is ample incentive for the public to seriously listen to the conservative alternatives being presented through the Republican Party.

It is a common tactic of policy advocates to invoke value-laden rhetoric to solicit support for policies designed to do little more than preserve longstanding political power structures. Today's liberal rhetoric, while seemingly not popular, is designed to reassure the public that something is being done to reduce crime through prevention. Similarly, while the conservative jargon is currently popular, tougher sentencing offers little substantive evidence that this approach will put a serious dent in crime.

The rhetorical debate between liberals and conservatives is fought tactically by applying both coercion and consensus techniques. For most of the last thirty years, crime policy at the national level has been dominated by the consensus tactic. Both liberals and conservatives, by necessity, must be in favor of measures to curb crime. It is inconceivable to imagine a political candidate running on either a "there is no crime in America" or "there is nothing government can do about crime" platform.

Thus, there is a great deal of incentive for politicians of different ideologies to reach a consensus that something should be done. Traditionally, this has involved a give-and-take cooperative strategy followed by a consensus-building tactic to close the policy deal. The 1994 crime bill is in many respects a throwback to the traditional consensus approach giving both liberals and conservatives some programs each wanted—to show the public that Congress could accomplish something with respect to what had become the number one issue in America (Gimpel, 1996).

However, the New Republican majority, under the tutelage of former Speaker of the House Newt Gingrich and a strong conservative wing, have shown increasing signs of unwillingness to compromise. If the principles of the new Republican majority are so sacred as to not be compromised under any circumstances, the only way the conservatives can implement their plans is through some sort of coercion tactic. Coercion need not be heavy-handed arm twisting to be effective. Several of the more common coercion tactics include invoking public opinion polls, previous election results, or impending elections as political leverage. In each situation, the coercive threat is the wrath of the public if opponents do not fall dutifully in line with the supposed dominant way of thinking.

The coercive tactic has, at best, proven to be effective in only the short term. The policy advocate forces the hand of adversaries when following the coercion tactic and risks complete rejection of his or her authority and prolonged gridlock. However, if backed into a corner, the policy advocate may feel that the rewards outweigh the risks (Fiorina, 1996).

One of three outcomes follows from coercive tactics: policy advocates succeed and their opponents are either converted or acquiesce for fear of retribution (in other words, losing the next election) if they continue to oppose the waves of change; opponents refuse to bend and stalemate and gridlock emerges. The risk with this result is that the policy advocate's political power is reduced. However, this reduction in power may be seen as worth the risk if it is calculated that the opponents also are unable to increase their power, that is, to keep the opponents at bay. While not the ideal solution, an opponent's loss of power is better than the alternative. This second outcome relies heavily on rhetoric and propaganda to be successful. The policy advocate must be able to convince the public that no policy change is better than going back to a failed policy (Bachrach and Baratz, 1970).

The power play of the policy advocate could fail. In this third outcome, opponents of the policy proposal in essence call the opponent's bluff. The policy advocate overplays the level of public support and demand for change resulting in the failure of the policy proposal. If the coercive battle is severe and prolonged, the failure could be compounded in that the policy advocate risks losing his political power base as well as the policy. That is, winning the next election could be seriously in jeopardy.

Thus, it is with great calculation and caution that decision makers employ the coercion tactic. The preferred course of action is normally to remain low key and seek incremental progress toward policy objectives through consensus-building techniques such as logrolling (you vote for my bill, I'll vote for yours). But if the stakes are high and ideology is more important to the policy advocate than marginal progress, the coercion tactic is the only viable alternative. Few elected officials or bureaucrats have the political will to undertake this all-or-nothing tactic, and decision makers are too vulnerable and too easily exposed. However, if successful, the rewards are often astronomical; but in this game, there are only clear winners and losers. If the policy advocate fails, defeat is normally accompanied by a significant loss of political power and potentially even the loss of legitimate power manifested in the form of major party defeats in the next election.

IDENTIFYING POLICY ADVOCATES BY
THEIR STRATEGIES AND TACTICS

When policy advocates combine a strategy with a tactic, they reveal their philosophies, or personalities, towards politics. Each policy advocate employs a particular strategy and tactic to optimize his or her perceived role in the political arena. Some policy advocates see themselves as elites who are better informed and equipped to lead. Others see the political arena as pluralist in nature, where any and all participants not only should be granted access to government but also receive a benefit. Still others see government as the avenue through which to promote a cause. These idealists, or ideologues, seek only to legitimize their own "correct" viewpoints. Finally, there are political participants who are more interested in playing the game than pursuing any particular policy outcome. These gamers, or economizers if you will, see policy more as a contest between consenting players where determining clear winners and losers is more central to politics than the adoption of a particular policy.

While this chapter is intended to be a general overview of theories of how government works, we discuss more thoroughly the role of elitism versus pluralism as driving forces in the policy process. Elites seek to gain and maintain controlling power over policy through the use of a combination of subtle coercion and cooperation. When policy advocates invoke a cooperative strategy, the intent is to reassure potential adversaries that there is nothing to fear by turning control of power and policy over to a narrow set of interests. Cooperation is essential to the elite strategy; for the elite to maintain control, they must convey to the public that the decision-making process is open and inclusive.

However, the power elite cannot control policy over the long term without making sure that political opponents and policy alternatives are kept in check (Bachrach and Baratz, 1970). To encourage cooperation, elite political actors employ the coercion tactic. As discussed earlier, the coercion devices are often subtle and soft, not harsh and heavy handed. Elites do not want to be exposed as an exclusive "members only" club or they risk exposure to an angry public.

To reassure nonelites that alternative voices do indeed make a difference in the direction of policy, elites rely heavily on rhetoric and symbolic gestures

(Edelman, 1985). Family values, the American dream, the Bill of Rights, and occasional references to "sweeping reform" are dished up by elites as evidence that policy is moving towards the overall protection of the public interest and not simply a reflection of a narrow agenda (Wilcox, 1995). In short, what is good for the elite is good for the public. With respect to crime policy, elite political behavior is commonly observable. Rhetoric such as "our policy will take back the streets, hire more police, and encourage parental responsibility" have little impact on crime but serves elites as it reassures everyone that the public interest and welfare is being served.

Other policy advocates believe that government has an obligation not only to hear what any interest group has to say but also, in some form or degree, to implement the demands of every group. These policy advocates are pluralists and are quick to point out the slightest advantage or disadvantage of groups in the policy-making arena. For the pluralist, the ideal policy is one where everyone gets something he or she wants and then it necessarily follows that no one goes away unhappy (Lowi, 1979). Pluralists also employ cooperation as their primary strategy for policy action. Unlike elites, pluralists are genuinely interested in adapting some of the ideas of adversaries to solicit cooperation. For pluralists to prosper in government, the need to reach a consensus is paramount (Dahl, 1967).

If all participants agree to cooperate by allowing each policy advocate to gain by the political process, than reaching a consensus is fairly easy. Pluralist political beings are even willing to allow contradictory and adversarial positions to be passed into law so long as no one has been left out of the process. In other words, all participants have to be able to claim victory (Lowi, 1979). Pluralism was especially present in the 1994 crime bill. To muster the votes for passage, otherwise opposing interests signed onto a bill that toughened sentences on the one hand (three strikes and you're out) and yet at the same time provided funding for controversial prevention programs such as midnight basketball (Quirk and Hinchliffe, 1996).

A third political philosophy is revealed by observing the strategies and tactics of the ideologue. The staunch, unbending, and unyielding advocate by nature generates conflict. However, conflict can be the ideologue's only strategy since cooperation with adversaries is out of the question. Typically, the ideologue states a willingness to listen to others but makes it clear that in the end, opponents must turn to his way of thinking or the policy is unacceptable. Therefore, when the decision is about to be made, the only tactical position which the ideologue can operate from is to attempt coercion to achieve his or her way of thinking.

Unlike elites, the coercive devices of the ideologue are not subtle. The ideologue does not care about image. In fact, the ideologue prefers openness and embraces exposure of the source and the message itself. There is no reason to shy away from conflict if only one viewpoint is correct. Crime policy, from time to time, has had its share of ideology, but this strategy typically is not the norm. For the most part, crime policy has been dominated by a struggle between elites and pluralists over control of power and policy. Coercive threats such as open accusations, outright condemnation of government and society, and unwillingness to bend tend to isolate the ideologue from the political process. For instance, Jesse Jackson has a more liberal view of the world in which crime is a function of societal flaws, but he is not a serious policy player. Similarly, on the conservative side, there are the Rick Santorums of the world, who have a clearly defined agenda but little chance of seeing it adopted in its entirety even with a Republican Congress. Perhaps an even better example would be Lyndon LaRouche, who contends that a criminal is not just someone who commits criminal acts but anyone who thinks criminal thoughts. Such thoughts would include putting one's own interests and those of one's family above the interests of the country (King, 1989).

A final policy advocate type is that of the gamer. This view holds that politics and policy making is the result of the distribution of a finite amount of resources where competitors compete equally in a political market to make policy choices. In political science circles, this type of decision-making structure encompasses political economics, public choice or rational choice theory, and game theories. *(See,* for example, Mancur Olson, *The Logic of Collective Action,* 1971; probably the most famous rational choice work is Garret Hardin's *The Tragedy of the Commons,* 1968, which examines the nuances between business and consumer interests to define the "public good." Other related works include James Gwartney's *Economics: Private and Public Choice,* 1994; James Buchanan's *The Theory of Public Choice II,* 1984; and Anatol Rappoport's, *Fights, Games, and Debates, 1960.)* In essence, the gamer sees politics as a zero-sum game with clear winners and clear losers.

The victory in a democratic or representative structure is having equal access to play the game, not guaranteed results. Those with the best skills, arguments, resources, and political support win. Alternative viewpoints clearly lose, but respect the outcome because the decision was made in a fair and open arena where everyone plays the game applying the same universally accepted rules.

For some political scientists, this form of participation is the ideal mode from which democratic governmental structures ought to operate. Theodore Lowi (1979), for instance, calls for a return to a more "juridical" democracy, where rule of law is the guiding principle of policymaking. In essence, Lowi asserts that the goal of democratic and representative forms of government is simply to guarantee access and a level playing field where all views are respectfully heard and debated. The flaw in pluralism is that it not only guarantees access to decision makers but also expects results. The problem facing policymakers today is that few in government are willing to say no, and fewer participants are willing to accept no for an answer. Thus, the goal of democracy is to legitimize open debate, not to endorse every idea that comes along. The gamer political style is often more normative than operational. It can only work when political participants accept that the rules of the game are simply to participate, that someone will win, and that others will accept defeat having agreed to the rules when they entered onto the playing field.

Theodore Lowi condemns pluralism and proposes a return to "rule of law" or a more "juridical democracy." Lowi's basic premise is that government be respected as a forum for participation, not a wishing well that guarantees results. When government responds to the demands of all organized interests, pluralism results and demoralizes, if not cripples, democratic government. A more "juridical" democracy encourages both winners and losers. Defeat is acceptable because it occurred in a fair and open democratic process where access is guaranteed, not results.

Gamers are best studied and observed at the level of the individual. For instance, we can observe an individual member of Congress making rational calculations as to whether to vote for a bill and asking certain questions in arriving at a decision. What are the political benefits and costs of voting for or against a particular crime bill? Will I get reelected? How will my colleagues in the Congress respond if I vote one way or the other? Will my power in the legislature be enhanced or diminished? The gamer sees the policy setting as one of open conflict. The basic tactic is consensus—oriented in that all participants agree to the rules of engagement. Thus, the real issue is whether the policy outcome is reached in a fair and equitable manner. The assumption is that the desirable policy is one of rational, logical choice rather than being ideologically or politically based. The optimal policy choice surfaces through the conflict and consensus of the democratic game, which is based on clear rules of acquisition and enables participants to accurately measure the benefits and costs of policy decisions.

Crime issues are rarely addressed from a game theory or public choice approach. There is, of course, the famous prisoner's dilemma about whether to confess to a crime, which is often cited as the perfect example of choices made using a game theory approach. While the illustration clearly shows the choices accused criminals face when confronted with the decision of whether to confess to a crime, the study is more illustrative of game theory and not a prescription, in and of itself, for a better crime policy. (For an excellent discussion and description of how the prisoner's dilemma can be applied to public policy decision making, *see* Henry, 1995.)

But if Lowi is correct, perhaps public choice options can be little more than theoretical precisely because government today does not operate from a "rule of law" foundation so essential to the success of public choice or game theory approaches. If indeed crime issues are being tossed about between power elites, then government's inability to directly address crime is easily explained. Elites and pluralists are more concerned with position and power and less concerned with policy outcomes. In truth, one could argue that regardless of whether elites or pluralists control the political arena, policy choices are made grudgingly. In either the pluralist or elitist political setting (or ideological approach for that matter), there is little opportunity for a game strategy or public economic choice theory to produce an optimal crime policy. Instead, to the extent that game theory is applicable, strategies and tactics are more concerned with who wins and loses in power struggles rather than over policy choices, which are little more than a reflection of the struggle for power.

SUMMARY

In this chapter we have identified the myriad of participants who influence the crime policy arena. More significantly, we have analyzed the political participants or policy advocates from the perspective of four basic ways of influencing governmental decision making. Policy advocates adopt elite, pluralist, ideological, or rational choice political behavioral patterns. Each type of policy advocate can be identified by the strategies and tactics the advocate employs in the policy decision-making arena.

Effective participation in the crime issue also is contingent on having adequate resources such as money and a permanent office; the effective and expedient use of time; and expertise, both political and with respect to policy. Criminal justice practitioners, as well as students of crime policy, will be better equipped to become serious players in the policy-making process by better understanding how effective participation occurs in government. Additionally, armed with the knowledge of how a variety of policy advocates attempt to influence change, criminal justice practitioners can better communicate with decision makers and hopefully become more serious players in the policy process. Finally, at minimum, a better understanding of how special interests influence policy will assist students of crime policy and practitioners alike in coping with the implementation, evaluation, and revision of laws that may make little sense in practice, but a great deal of sense politically.

REVIEW QUESTIONS

1. Why are some special interests more influential in politics than others?
2. As a student and/or practitioner in criminal justice, discuss how you would distinguish between elites, pluralists, idealists, and rational actors. How would you, in the role of a criminal justice practitioner, deal with each type of political actor?
3. Identify the possible special interests involved in the issue presented at the beginning of this chapter.

Chapter Three

How Crime Policy Is Made

LEARNING OBJECTIVES

In this chapter, you will do the following:

1. Develop a framework for studying policy generally, and crime policy specifically
2. Distinguish between the process, politics, and science of policymaking
3. Discover how macro-level policy making affects the everyday work of criminal justice practitioners.
4. Explore specific techniques and tools for becoming an effective participant in the policy-making process

INTRODUCTION

At a basic level, it is difficult to understand why there is so much controversy surrounding the crime issue. Everyone agrees that crime is a problem, one that government should address. However, in the real world of policymaking, the debate is often over how to address a problem, not whether the problem exists. Crime is no exception. As we learned in the last chapter, there are many forms of participation and a variety of motivations for participating in the policy process. To sort through the complex web of political interests, students of policy need a practical framework of analysis that explains the complex interaction between political participants and the governmental process.

Several variations of the policy cycle have been developed in public policy literature. Probably the most noted framework is offered by Charles O. Jones, who identifies the sequential steps as agenda setting, policy formulation, legitimation, appropriation, policy implementation, and policy evaluation (Jones, 1984). Similar models have been developed by Brewer and de Leon (1983), James E. Anderson (1997), and James P. Lester and Joseph Stewart (1996). Brewer and de Leon begin with initiation, and substitute estimation and selection as part of their framework. Anderson includes revision and impact as part of policy evaluation. Lester and Stewart insert policy termination instead of policy revision, noting that either policy success or failure can lead to discontinuation of a policy.

In developing the framework for this text, we combine the insight of the more traditional public policy cycle models with systems analysis as designed by David Easton (1979b). Viewed as a system, the political process requires inputs, operations, outputs, and feedback to operate (Easton, 1979b). Political systems operate much like a machine requiring an energy supply (inputs), a mechanism (governmental operations), outputs (an end product), and feedback (assessment of the mechanism's efficiency and effectiveness). While not all input sources are equal at all times, the demands of a political system are expressed through elections, political parties, special interests, the media, and public opinion; all illustrate the energy supply or "inputs" needed to get the governmental process started.

The government operations stage represents the engine at work turning and churning to produce policy. Outputs are the policies government produces that are implemented to serve society or the needs of interest groups. Finally, feedback includes policy evaluation, impact, and revision. Our approach is to combine the policy cycle perspectives with a systems perspective to produce a simplified, four-step approach to understanding how the governmental process works and the impact of that process on policy development. We introduced the model in Chapter 1 and we now present it in greater detail.

AGENDA SETTING: GETTING THE PROBLEM TO GOVERNMENT

A vital ingredient to starting government's engine is the allocation of resources towards finding and opening government's access points. Kingdon (1995) argues that certain process streams must come together for policy changes to occur. These streams of problems, policies, and politics are largely independent; once coupled, a policy window opens that allows, or facilitates, policy change. Thus, in the same way that oil is converted to gas, which finds its way into your automobile's gas tank via the gas pump, citizens must find a way to couple at least two of the process streams to convert demands into solutions that government can store for later use. Once the issue, and its accompanying solution, reaches the institutional agenda, the issue receives attention. In a democratic/representative form of government, the fuel sources that propel issues onto the institutional agenda include: elections, organized special interests, political parties, the media, public opinion, expertise, and government officials. These sources of inputs or demands set the general tone of debate under which government will operate.

But not all of these sources of demands are equally effective. Recall Chapter 2, where we pointed out that, the effectiveness of participation is greatly dependent on time, resources, and expertise. Where all three are present in a political participant, there is a greater likelihood of successfully getting on the government's systemic agenda—that is, the opportunity to be placed with all the other issues the political community perceives to deserve attention and be within the legitimate jurisdiction of government. The more broadly undefined an issue or demand, the more likely the issue will remain a part of the institutional agenda—that is, kept in the background as merely a discussion item waiting to find a permanent (systemic) place in the governmental arena (Cobb and Elder, 1983).

Once on the systemic agenda, policy participants actively seek to promote their own policies but also keep the opposition confined to the institutional agenda. These two faces of power are vital to understanding who wins and loses in the policy process (Bachrach and Baratz, 1970). Too often, students of policy observe obviously visible tactics such as lobbying and campaign funding as merely tools for getting on the agenda, while ignoring that these resources also work to systematically keep competing interests at bay. From this perspective, it is clear that participants in agenda setting are not necessarily playing on a level field.

Public opinion expressed through elections and polls is at best a means of molding the discussion agenda. Long-term influence or residence in the systemic agenda is greatly dependent on possessing adequate resources. Thus, interest groups, issue experts, and even government officials have the upper hand during agenda setting. Their common thread of power is time, money, and expertise. This political context demonstrates that control over the policy agenda normally comes from within governmental circles and not from the general public.

It is not enough to simply grab government's ear. The policy cycle reveals that complaints and complainers are commonly long on rhetoric and short on substantive solutions. The politics of agenda setting is about getting government to listen over the long term. The key to getting government's attention is in reality quite simple. Those participants who are taken seriously are able to present themselves in the government arena in a credible and capable way. They can answer very basic questions relevant to most if not all issues including crime. What is your solution to the problem and is it realistically attainable? Policy advocates who can answer this question have a leg up on those who cannot. It is one thing to complain about government inaction or a problem facing society, it is entirely another matter to have a workable remedy for what is ailing the country.

The nature of the issue is also important for reaching the agenda. A number of questions about the issue must be answered if it is to be placed on the agenda: (1) Is it a trendy issue? (2) Does it have a wide impact? (3) Is, or was, the issue precipitated by a triggering event such as the Oklahoma City bombing? (4) Does it involve power perceived as unfairly used?

If you approach government with a problem but without a viable solution, then government is not likely to address it. In many respects, the unspoken requirement of a viable or credible plan serves a gate-keeping function, separating the serious policy makers from the more common, uninformed, complaining public.

POLICY FORMULATION—DEVELOPMENT OF ALTERNATIVES

Policy formulation is the stage in the policy process where attainable and workable plans of action are identified, debated, and negotiated in governmental institutions, particularly within Congress at the national government level and the legislature in state government (Lester and Stewart, 1996). But how do we define attainable and workable? By what criteria can we determine whether a policy actor has developed a viable option for addressing a problem or issue?

A common approach is to argue the merits of the option on scientific grounds or past experiences. These solutions are analogous to policies that have been enacted by alternative governmental bodies (Anderson, 1997). For instance, in our federal system, states have constitutional authority to enact laws independent of national policy making. In the area of crime, a noteworthy example is that some states have the death penalty for first degree murder while other states have life imprisonment. Arguments for and against the death penalty are then extrapolated by the evidence available at the state level.

Another analogous approach is to compare nations. One statistic often played with is the high murder rate in the United States compared to the relatively low murder rates of countries such as Canada and Great Britain, both of which have strict gun control laws. Still another option is to appeal directly to the decision makers on policies they know best, namely laws currently in place. If alterations can be presented that are incremental yet offer the possibility of significant results, a policy alternative has a better opportunity to be seriously addressed.

Creative and new proposals are rarely successful during policy formulation. An entirely new approach seldom carries with it a significant body of evidence to calm the fears decision makers develop over rapid and sweeping change. Incrementalism is the preferred course of action. Slow but steady progress over a long period of time is a much easier sell to decision makers. In addition, marginal changes in policy allow for reflection and alteration as conditions in the environment change (Lindblom, 1959). The assumption is that it is easier to correct small errors than large mistakes (Wildavsky, 1979). Minor adjustments in policies are less costly and less obtrusive in individuals' lives. The skilled policy formulator not only understands the value of incrementalism and the issue, but also the political environment in which the policy must traverse.

Still another way to examine policy formation is to observe not only the methods for getting government to act but also the efforts to prevent items from being placed on the agenda. Sometimes referred to as non-decision making, the intent is to sufficiently discredit an alternative to the point that it is never seriously considered as a viable issue or problem (Bachrach and Baratz, 1970). A non-decision-making strategy can be used to protect an existing policy. It also can be a means for keeping alternative approaches from being seriously considered if your own demands are also under scrutiny and attack.

Policy formulation requires a plan of action and a strategy for seeing it through to adoption. Some would seek to sell a plan simply on its merits. This "perfect plan," however, is subject to the political pressures influencing the issue. Elites will challenge the notion of the perfect plan in at least two ways. Either the preferred plan is already operating, or the proposed "perfect plan" is too adventurous, risky, untested, and extreme. In a pluralist setting, the perfect plan is bargained over and compromised to accommodate as many interests as possible with the least amount of pain or cost.

Ideologues are unlikely to see their definition of a perfect plan enacted because opponents will criticize its narrow thinking and the idealists themselves will be unwilling to compromise any aspect of the plan to get it passed. Only in a "gaming" political environment where rule-of-law is accepted can the perfect plan have a chance of passage solely on its merits. For in the rule-of-law setting, a plan that can muster majority support would easily pass. Adversaries willingly accept defeat on the grounds that the prize is participation, not results.

As we discussed in the previous chapter, the American political system at present resists a more rule-bound, game-type of political environment. Scholars contend that the American political system is elitist, pluralist, or a combination of the two. Regardless of where one defines politics along the elitist-pluralist spectrum, it is clear that the merits of a plan have only a marginal impact in either political setting. What is effective is the development and use of strategies and tactics for influencing the political realm of elites (if you subscribe to the elite theory) or pluralists (if you subscribe to pluralism). In both political arenas, a premium is placed on who you know, how you pique their interests, and ultimately how to close the policy deal. The perfect strategy for action is as important, if not more so, than the plan itself.

In essence, the perfect strategy is often more effective in assisting a policy actor in traversing the policy cycle than the perfect plan or proposal itself. In fact, once a policy option enters into the political fray, it is quickly understood that there is no such thing as a perfect plan. The perfect plan is constantly bombarded by ideological, philosophical, and partisan differences. In spite of ever-growing mounds of research and statistical data, social and political options are open to interpretation since they are often driven far more by emotions and beliefs then by quantifiable measurable variables.

In the ideal world, the perfect plan and perfect strategy would blend together to produce widely acceptable remedies to problems. But in the realm of institutions controlled by humans, arguments of merit often take a back seat to what is politically expedient. Thus, more often than not, the perfect understanding of the strategies and tactics essential to traversing the policy process is far more important than having developed the perfect plan. This is especially true if it assumed that there is no such thing as the "perfect" policy option.

Recall that the major tenet of agenda setting is "no viable solution or remedy, no problem." The term *viable* is the key to unlocking the door to policy formulation. Viability is more than an idea or plan and includes a keen understanding of politics, key political players, and the policy-making environment. This is why identifying and recognizing the four policy environments identified in Chapter 2 are so essential to effectively participating in the policy process.

Unless one's strategic and tactical awareness of the political environment is well developed, all of the best-laid plans in the world have little chance of moving beyond the input stage of the policy cycle. To be part of the policy formulation team, and ideally a key player throughout the policy cycle, policy actors must be skilled practitioners of the policy process as well as in their field of study. Thus, for criminal justice practitioners, it is not enough to collect data and reflect intellectually about crime. Criminal justice practitioners only can be effective in the political process when their commitment to understanding the political process is as great as their commitment to the study of crime issues and the field of criminal justice.

INSTITUTIONAL DECISION MAKING—THE PROCESS OF POLICY ADOPTION

Of the four steps of the policy cycle, government action is probably the most recognizable aspect of the policy-making process. If there is one area where students are exposed to the inner workings of government, it is in the area of how the American government is structured and operates. From the grade school civics lesson to the college-level government course, basic training is offered in how Congress, the executive branch, and the judiciary conduct their daily business.

Our purpose here is not to repeat detailed descriptions of a process so readily available in standard government texts. The focus is on those factors that are significant to sustaining involvement throughout the policy cycle, and in this particular instance, the politics of the governmental action or decision-making stage. The focus is on three particular components of national decision making: (1) the power of committees in Congress, (2) the power of presidential persuasion, and (3) the role of the Supreme Court in the judicial setting. Criminal justice practitioners need to understand the perspectives, roles, and powers of national decision makers to more fully comprehend the nuances of legislation they are ultimately asked to implement.

CONGRESSIONAL DECISION MAKING

With respect to how Congress makes a decision, the most important level of analysis is found in the various standing committees. All legislation is funneled at the committee level. Subcommittee government continues to be essential to the legislative process. Nevertheless, power has devolved to freshmen legislators, and committee chairs have been neutered to a degree. The power of the committee is expressed in its authority to hold hearings and invoke testimony from individuals and groups for and against legislation. The committees have the authority to amend and mark up a bill as they see fit. Standing committees have the authority to vote up or down on a bill. If the bill is voted down, it normally dies in the committee, never to be voted on by the House or Senate. The House and Senate as a whole can force a bill out of committee only by a discharge petition. Even then, these bills only can be debated on the second or fourth Monday of each month Congress is in session. Further, in the House, signatures of an absolute majority (218) are required to bring a bill out of committee to a vote. Thus, it is extremely difficult to undo a decision made by a standing committee (Davidson and Oleszek, 1981).

Once the House and Senate pass a bill, the legislation usually must go to a conference committee made up of members of both the House and Senate. Typically, the give-and-take of bargaining in the House and Senate creates a situation where both chambers have passed two different versions of the same bill. These differences must be ironed out in conference. Before an act can be sent on to the president for signature or veto, every item from dollar amounts to specific wording must be the same in both the House and Senate versions. If the House and Senate conferees cannot agree as to the content of the bill, then the bill dies in spite of the months of previous gut-wrenching negotiations within each chamber. Still, even if the conferees come to agreement as to the particulars of the bill, that version must be approved one final time by the full House and Senate (Davidson and Oleszek, 1981).

Another important revelation about how Congress works under the committee system is in the nature and scope of the political ties individual members of Congress develop as members of a standing committee. Committees in Congress are set up to deal with broad issue areas. For instance, there are committees on agriculture, the judiciary, defense, interior, and so on. Members of Congress spend most of their time becoming familiar with a select set of issues and subsequently a select set of interests.

Political science literature refers to this network of players as a "subgovernmental system." A more commonly recognized phrase describing this type of politics is the "iron triangle" (Anderson, 1997). The iron triangle refers to the relationship between congressional committee members, special interests, and administrative agencies who share a common interest in a particular issue.

Iron triangles assist in explaining the presence of "pork barrel" legislation. Pork barrel projects such as water projects, placement of highways, city services, and location of defense-related plants and bases is a way for an individual member of Congress to directly assist constituencies at little or no cost to those benefiting from the project since overall tax revenues are used to provide a service to a select group of people. It is assumed that without government "pork," there would not be enough local capital to bring about the creation of the specific item funded. Iron triangles and pork barrel legislation had its heyday from the 1930s to the 1960s. More recently, as federal budgets tightened and as interest groups have proliferated since 1970, it has become increasingly difficult for iron triangles to operate without significant opposition (Fiorina, 1996).

In response to the seemingly inadequate and oversimplified concept of the iron triangle, Hugh Heclo developed the concept of the issue network (Heclo, 1978). The primary difference between the issue network and the iron triangle is the level of open competition for government's attention during policy making. Heclo recognizes the specialization of committees and government agencies, but expands the involvement of special interests to include advocates and opponents of a policy.

A one-time classic example of the iron triangle was agriculture and the subsidy program. Today, agriculture is no longer simply a family farm issue. In response to an ever-growing agricultural economy, Congress now attempts to balance the demands of corporate producers, trade business, retail groceries, and a host of other characters that are often lumped together under the umbrella of "agribusiness."

The evolution of the iron triangle to issue network is also relevant to understanding crime issues. It was once thought that the National Rifle Association (NRA) had captured all relevant decision makers in Congress regarding the issue of gun control. In the last several years, the NRA has suffered a series of setbacks ranging from the Brady Bill to the 1994 crime bill, which included a ban on assault weapons, to financial problems. They remain, however, an effective interest group. A number of effectively organized special interests with an adversarial relationship oppose the NRA. They range from police organizations, which are increasingly frustrated with confronting well-armed criminals, to citizen activist groups (Spitzer, 1995).

Analyzing the decentralized nature of the committee system reveals several important facets of the decision-making process in Congress. First, multiple policy-making settings provide access for many groups and interests. The decentralized nature of Congress makes it very difficult for any single interest to dominate the legislative process. However, the decentralized nature of Congress makes it easier to block the enactment of legislation seen as counter or hostile to a dominant group's policy preferences or positions (Anderson, 1997).

Second, the decentralized process puts a premium on bargaining, negotiation, compromise, and incrementalism—assuming the goal is to pass legislation. Ideological participants are easily frustrated by a process that demands compromise to build the consensus needed for a majority vote. But the ideologue takes some solace and comfort in knowing that a decentralized system of subgovernment makes it easier to block the enactment of legislation counter to the philosophies of the idealist. Thus, the "gridlock" we hear so much about in the press as being a Democratic versus Republican problem is in many respects built into the system (Fiorina, 1996). The legislative process is for the most part about debate and to prevent the adoption of nutty ideas. The fact that in the last thirty years government produced huge budgets and deficits reflects a willingness to compromise that is in some respects quite remarkable.

The gridlock strategy employed to deal with budget and deficit issues in the nineties merely reflects those aspects of the process designed to legitimately block legislation. Gridlock has always been an option. For nearly thirty-five years of massive government spending both parties chose to compromise in the name of "good" government; whereas, in the nineties, both parties chose to compromise to balance the budget, also in the name of "good" government.

PRESIDENTIAL EFFORT TO INFLUENCE POLICY

Presidential efforts in decision making are almost entirely informal. Perhaps the only real power presidents have over decision makers is the power of persuasion (Neustadt, 1990). If presidents relied solely on powers explicitly written into the Constitution, the only significant role for the executive would be to read the act and decide whether to sign or veto the work of Congress. In contemporary politics, this passive approach has become unacceptable to presidents and the public. As the only nationally elected official, presidents see their role as one of guiding the national policy agenda. Presidents serve to remind individual members of Congress that the U.S. Congress is a national institution that needs to respond to national and international events as well as local concerns. In this capacity, the president is only as effective as his ability to persuade through symbols, rhetoric, the credibility of the office, the use of the bully pulpit, and the occasional threat.

Compared to the structured and complex world of Congress, presidents operate in a power vacuum. Congress holds the purse strings, drafts the bills, debates the merits of the legislation, and decides the immediate fate of all legislation. For the executive officer to influence the decision-making process, the president must seize political opportunities to enhance his power. Politically, power in Washington floats from individual to individual based on their credibility, leadership skills, and political prowess (Smith, 1988).

Presidents, and governors at the state level, must look for weaknesses or vulnerabilities in the congressional (or legislature) leadership and seize opportunities to influence the national or state agenda and subsequent decision making. The rapid ebb and flow of power to and from the president was readily apparent in the Clinton presidency. On the one hand, the president was able to rally special interests and the public around the issue of crime and pass the 1994 crime bill. On the other hand, President Clinton was unable to muster the same level of support to get health care legislation through Congress. This illustrates that policy can take on a life of its own; in the case of health care, it became too cerebral to remain salient and perhaps also fell victim to partisan politics (Johnson and Broder, 1996).

In stark contrast are daily visual, graphic, and simple-to-comprehend reminders of the never-ending crime story. The litany of violent crimes routinely spewed forth on television news above all other stories keeps crime in the forefront of governmental activities. In many respects, the complexity of the crime issue is just as great as that of health care or any other identifiable issue. The difference is that crime takes little time or few resources for news services to cover. Crime also has the advantage of being visually graphic and therefore an immediate attention grabber for the television-viewing audience.

Thus, presidential policy initiatives are guided less by ideas and more by passion (Neustadt, 1990). Presidents must be able to persuade Congress to take action. Rarely are presidents able to move Congress without solid support of the public, the president's party, interest groups, and an attentive media (Wayne, 1996). Effective presidents understand that the perception of power is all that matters. Ronald Reagan and his advisors, for instance, chose battles carefully, limiting fights to issues where strong support already existed. President Clinton, on the other hand, has not been so selective or as effective (Campbell and Rockman, 1996).

Crime is an issue that arouses the passions of voters, no matter what their political party affiliation. While the specifics of dealing with crime can be very controversial (for example, gun control), any president can grab the public's ear instantly by simply using the bully pulpit of the presidency. It would be misleading to suggest that passing a crime bill through Congress is an easy task. The Brady Bill floundered throughout the Reagan and Bush presidencies, and Clinton's crime bill passed by the narrowest of margins. But most presidential initiatives are met with skepticism by Congress. What makes the crime issue attractive to presidents is that it is a problem that always seems in need of attention and the public always seems interested in seeing that crime is attended to.

One final point here, and that is the issue of individual agencies having the ability to select crimes that they want to focus law enforcement efforts on. For example, former Attorney General Janet Reno made domestic violence and hate crime a priority. In 1993, the director of the FBI diverted resources from espionage to street gangs to assist local jurisdictions in their efforts. In 2005, the focus has shifted to terrorism and related activities. Thus, at the federal level, the Federal Bureau of Investigation, the Drug Enforcement Agency, the Immigration and Customs Enforcement Agency all have some discretion in the direction of their efforts.

THE SUPREME COURT AS POLICYMAKER

Since the Warren Court of the 1960s, the Supreme Court of the United States
has come under increasing attack as being too much involved in policy making rather than fulfilling its role as interpreter of the law and the Constitution.
Nowhere has this controversy been more apparent than in the crime issue.
The *Miranda* warnings and the search warrant requirement are both products
of 1960s Supreme Court decisions relating to the Bill of Rights and the rights
of citizens when confronted by law enforcement officials. Subsequently,
more conservative Courts have added exceptions to these rules, reflecting
public concern that the judicial process overly protected the criminal at the
expense of the defenseless victim.

Our intention here is not to reexamine this controversy, but rather to
demonstrate how the Supreme Court makes decisions and in general address
whether it is realistic to expect any Supreme Court (liberal, conservative, or
moderate) to not influence the policy-making process. Politics is built into
the operation of the Supreme Court and the federal court system more generally. In other words, the federal judicial process, as much as the individuals wearing the robes, makes it highly unlikely that the Court can ever be
completely devoid of politics and policy making. Thus, procedures such as
the *Miranda* warnings and the search warrant requirement are as much about
striking a balance between political viewpoints as they are about constitutional principles.

To illustrate the policy-making power of the Supreme Court, consider the
concept of justice. Seemingly a simple enough idea, few can argue that justice is a principal goal of the American judicial process. Yet, justice in practice has proven to be extremely controversial. In the contemporary setting,
debate centers on the rights of the accused versus protection of the rights of
victims (society). We are now involved in a thirty-year debate dating back to
the Warren Court. Recent Supreme Court nominations in part have been in response to the concern that liberal policies have overly protected the criminal
at the expense of innocent victims and society's "right" to punish offenders.
The more conservative approach has produced, for example, a number of exceptions to search warrants including the "good faith" exception (O'Brien,
1990).

The examination of the crime issue from a policy perspective reveals that
a consensus on what is justice is not likely to be forthcoming any time soon
for three reasons. The first is the inability of constitutional and legal scholars
to come to a uniform agreement as to the role of the Court in political issues
such as social reform, economic regulation, and civil liberties, to name a few.
Second, justice in the United States revolves around a political process for se-

lecting judges and the exercise of judicial power that works against the courts as objective, third-party interpreters of the Constitution (O'Brien, 1990).

Finally, the public appears split on the notion of what the role of the judicial branch is in their lives and what constitutes justice. On the one hand, the individual citizen concedes the need to protect the innocent from false accusation. On the other hand, the public is insistent that the criminal be punished swiftly and surely as retribution for crimes committed against society (Bonser et al, 1996).

The inability of scholars, politicians, and the public to agree on what is meant by justice creates a legal cloud and encourages errors to creep into what otherwise would be the most apolitical and unbiased of all branches of government. Even well-intended humans capable of sound reasoning make mistakes without the help of legal doctrine. Adapting a legal system that presumes one type of error is more likely to occur or be preferred over another only serves to legitimize error over reason.

To illustrate natural error in any legal issue, all one needs to do is examine the possible outcomes in any given case. In simplified form, any trial is about guilt or innocence. In this ideal state, there is no question of whether or when justice is served. However, when one considers that it is possible that the wrong decision is reached, the image of the legal world changes from yes or no to maybe — with the maybe reflecting the possibility that the legal system has imprisoned an innocent individual or allowed a guilty person to go free.

Figure 3.1 illustrates the possible outcomes in matrix form. Justice is clearly served when a jury reaches the correct decision by either putting a guilty person in jail or finding an innocent person not guilty. However, when a wrong decision is reached, an error has occurred. The question facing policymakers and specifically the U.S. Supreme Court is whether one error is preferable over another. In a Type I error, an innocent person is found guilty. In a Type II error, a guilty person is set free. The issues are whether one type of error is constitutionally preferred over the other, whether the Court should follow social or public preference and create rules and procedures to promote the popular choice, or whether neither error is worthy of concern as long as each error occurs seldom and randomly (Bonser et al., 1996).

The more liberal courts of the sixties and seventies looked carefully at a hundred years of neglect in the areas of civil rights, gender discrimination, and the legal rights of the poor, and set into motion a number of procedures to discourage wrongful punishments. The assumption of liberal justices over the last thirty years is that the legal system has been stacked against the individual and the innocent. Because of the powers so easily brought to bear on government in the form of societal pressure and wealth, liberals believe that

	Accused is guilty	Accused is innocent
Found Guilty	Correct	Incorrect Innocent put in jail
Found Not Guilty	Incorrect Guilty set free	Correct

In any trial there are four possible outcomes. There is more at stake than simply finding a person guilty or innocent. It is also possible the wrong decision is made. In such instances, there are two possibilities. Either a guilty person is found innocent and is set free, or an innocent person is found guilty and punished. It is the recognition of possible human error that guides legal thinking and more specifically the Supreme Court's concern over balancing the rights of the individual accused of a crime and the rights of the victim and more broadly society to see that justice is served. The Miranda Warnings and the Search Warrant are two examples of how the Supreme Court has attempted to reduce the chances of committing the error of putting an innocent person in jail. The various Exceptions to Search Warrants (and efforts to allow admission of confessions into court even though the defendant may not have been read his/her rights) address the second error, the possibility that a guilty person is set free on a technicality. Liberal judges are traditionally more concerned with preventing the imprisonment of an innocent person. Conservative judges are more likely to push for rules and procedures which increase convictions in the effort to protect innocent victims of crime. Which position would you rather be in as an innocent individual, Innocent and in jail, or the innocent victim with the criminal set free? How confident are you that a jury, attorneys, judges, and the legal system never make a mistake? If you were wrongly accused of a crime, which error would you want the courts to recognize as a distinct possibility?

Figure 3.1.   Trial and Error

the *Miranda* warnings and strict supervision of search warrants are necessary to protect those with few resources (O'Brien, 1990). On the other had, conservative justices (and members of Congress) assert that those decisions limit the ability of law enforcement to curb crime and terrorism effectively.

The conservative movement counters the liberal view by arguing that a woeful neglect of the rights of innocent victims has occurred. Instead, liberal justice produces a legal system that not only protects the wrongly accused but in doing so promotes the release of clearly guilty individuals.

In any trial there are four possible outcomes. There is more at stake than simply finding a person guilty or innocent. It is also possible the wrong decision is made. In such instances, there are two possibilities. Either a guilty person is found innocent and is set free (Type I Error), or an innocent person is found guilty and is punished (Type II Error). The recognition of possible human error guides legal thinking and more specifically the Supreme Court's concern over balancing the rights of the individual accused of a crime and the rights of the victim and more broadly society to see that justice is served.

The *Miranda* warnings and the search warrant are two examples of how the Supreme Court has attempted to reduce the chances of committing the error of putting an innocent person in jail. The various exceptions to search warrants (and efforts to allow admission of confessions into court even though the defendant may not have been read his or her rights) address the second error, the possibility that a guilty person is set free on a technicality. Liberal judges are traditionally more concerned with preventing the imprisonment of an innocent person. Conservative judges are more likely to push for rules and procedures which increase convictions to protect innocent victims of crime. Which position would you rather be in as an innocent individual—innocent and in jail, or the innocent victim with the criminal set free? How confident are you that a jury, attorneys, judges, and the legal system never make a mistake? If you were wrongly accused of a crime, which error would you want the courts to recognize as a distinct possibility?

Type I error produces a bias in judicial outcomes. Yet, overly protecting societal interests increases the chances of putting an innocent person behind bars. Thus, the conservative position taken to the extreme promotes a Type II error. Unless decision makers and the public uniformly agree that either a Type I error or a Type II error is indeed the preferred definition of justice, both errors fail to meet the test of neutrality (Bonser et al., 1990).

A policy cycle perspective reveals the difficulty of separating the politics from process in the legislative, executive, and judicial relationship. Within the last ten years especially, the Senate and the president have engaged in some heated debates over the politics of Supreme Court nominations, epitomized by the failed Bork nomination (O'Brien, 1990). In fact, the battle to seat Judge Bork introduced a new word into the American lexicon-"borked"-meaning to be viciously and slanderously attacked. Accusations of playing politics with an appointment supposedly free of politics has become commonplace. Scholars and politicians alike have called for appointment of judges who interpret rather than legislate. However, the fact remains that so long as liberal and conservative thinking is at odds over the direction of error built into the legal system, it is unlikely that any federal justice, liberal or conservative, will ever be seen simply as an interpreter of law. Chief Justice John Roberts and Justice Samuel Alito recent confirmation hearings demonstrate the contentious struggle over the Supreme Court's ideological makeup. Along the path of getting Roberts and Alito confirmed, Harriet Miers had her candidacy vetoed over her perceived softeness as a true "conservative."

Needless to say, the inability of either the political or legal arenas to define the parameters of what constitutes American justice puts criminal justice practitioners in a precarious situation when implementing public policies produced by the Congress and the president, and when carrying out the legal procedures imposed by the Supreme Court. In this context we turn to the output cell of the policy cycle, or policy implementation.

POLICY OUTPUTS

Simply speaking, implementation is "getting the job done." Implementation involves carrying out law(s) enacted during policy adoption. Implementation is usually studied as either a process, an output, or in terms of outcomes (Lester and Stewart, 1996). Each approach brings a unique perspective to improving an understanding of implementation. Implementation as process emphasizes the importance of public administration, organization, and management in the policy setting. Output studies reveal whether policies reach intended publics. Examination of outcomes addresses whether implemented policies make a measurable difference on targeted problems (Mazmanian and Sabatier, 1983).

PROCESS

Process involves the establishment of some sort of administrative component to oversee the implementation process. Most policies in the United States are implemented through the executive branches of national, state, and local government. The reliance on administration for the implementation of policy has spawned a large bureaucracy where agencies have a great deal of discretionary power to carry out policies under their jurisdiction as they see fit, as long as agency actions fall within the general parameters or intent set up by authorizing legislation. Thus, the bureaucratic component of government is a key factor in the implementation process.

Bureaucracy becomes institutionalized because government cannot carry out its policies without using the skills and expertise of professionals commonly referred to as bureaucrats—who work in executive departments, offices, and agencies. The authority of agencies and departments are further enhanced by rule-making and procedural powers granted by law in recognition of the highly technical skills and expertise of public officials. In essence, agencies have the power not only to implement policy but also to make additions to policy, which have the force of law. When Congress appears only to be able to address issues in the broadest of contexts, agencies are asked to step in and provide the specifics.

When legislators are either unable or unwilling to attend to the details of governance, bureaucracies not only are created but institutionalized. The organizational environment of bureaucracy can have a significant impact on implementation. Let us examine bureaucracy more closely. A bureaucracy is sufficiently large so that the highest levels of management seldom (if ever) have direct contact with the lowest level employees. A bureaucracy also has specialized jurisdictions in response to the ever-expanding and technically complex nature of problems addressed by government. Additionally, a bureaucracy typically establishes top-down lines of authority. General policy decisions are made at the higher levels of administration whereas specific tasks of implementation are assigned to lower-level employees (Henry, 1995).

The operating environment of government bureaucracy illustrates one benefit of studying implementation as process. Bureaucracy influences implementation separately from politics, society, or other forces. For instance, an entire body of literature has emerged examining the relationship between employee's personalities and behaviors in large organizations.

Box 3.1 provides the opportunity to match personality with behaviors. Public personnel and organizational management research reveals how factors internal to the organization can work against effective implementation as well as enhance an agency's work. In addition to observable behavioral patterns, large organizations use techniques such as Management by Objectives (MBO) to assist in the operations of the organization. Obviously, if the organization is unable to function properly, it becomes extremely difficult for implementation to occur no matter how well constructed the policy or law. These and other organizational factors will be examined in more detail in Part Two of this text.

Implementation observed from an output perspective is concerned with whether the law or policy was actually carried out. In crime policy, the analyst might observe how arrests are made, how *specific* criminal procedures are followed or to what extent the determinant sentence affects prison management. That is, the analyst studying policy output determines the extent designated procedures and policies are followed (Lester and Stewart, 1996).

Box 3.1. Personality Types in Large Organizations

**Recognizing and Dealing with
Patterns of Organizational Behavior**

Overview

Individuals in organizations or large institutions such as the executive branch are encouraged to adapt their behavior to reflect the values, procedures, and policies of the organization in which they work. At the same time it is quite common for individuals to respond differently to organizational patterns of behavior. Some individuals see the organization as an opportunity for self-improvement and advancement. Others see organizations as stifling and controlling. There are many identifiable patterns of organizational adaptation, two of which we examine.

Purpose

Studying patterns of adaptation allows managers in the public and private sectors to:

(a) design organizations that will promote preferred behavioral patterns;

(b) anticipate, understand, and respond appropriately to employee behaviors; and

(c) better assist employees in dealing with the bureaucratic nature of government.

Objectives

To identify and be able to discuss:

1. Six behavioral patterns observable in most any public or private organization.
2. Advantages and disadvantages of each personality type.

Personalities/Behaviors

(1–2, Alvin Gouldner; 3–6, Michael Maccoby)

1. Cosmopolitan: professional, field expert, emphasis on skill, lacks company loyalty, satisfaction in personal achievement over organizational success.
2. Local: nonprofessional, less skilled, organizationally functional, high job loyalty.
3. The Gamesman: sees life including work as a game to be won or lost.
4. The Craftsman: enjoys career, meticulous, emphasis on quality over quantity.
5. The Company Man: empathy, integrity, image of the office must be upheld.
6. The Jungle Fighter: sees only power struggles, worker rivalries, fights.

Activity

Assign a behavior/personality type to each of the following individuals.

1. Sam to Agency Head McBrain: "I know the report you asked for is late but I want to make sure every piece of information is accurate so that it reflects well on the quality of my work."
2. Deputy Director Skinner to staff: "When you work here you must wear a suit, be clean cut, and keep a neat work area at all times."
3. Park Ranger Smith to co-worker Jones: "Everyone knows the head ranger is retiring soon so just beware that every day, everything we do is just to see how the pecking order shakes out."
4. Police Officer Hall: "What I love most about what I do is that every day is a challenge to see who wins and who loses; regardless, it's fun to play, to take a gamble. It's no fun standing idle.
5. District Attorney Sheister: "When I took this job it was because I knew with my skills that I could make a difference in law, to the legal profession, to justice. I can do that anywhere."
6. Gray to Director White: "I'll go wherever you need me, accept any task you assign. The important thing I give the organization is my dedication. There's plenty around here who know everything."

Sources: Gouldner, 1978; Maccoby, 1978.

OUTCOMES

Outcomes relate to measuring changes that have occurred because of the law or program being implemented (Lester and Stewart, 1996). For example, the crime policy analyst observing outcomes is interested in determining whether the crime rate has declined because of a particular crime program or piece of legislation such as the "Three strikes and you're out" law. In this setting, policy implementation and evaluation become integrated activities.

Programs are analyzed in a larger context and may include outputs and process factors as partial influences on outcomes. Other factors considered would be political, social, and economic influences working to promote or thwart the implementation of policy. In essence, outcome studies recognize that implementation is the product of both internal and external forces.

The complex nature of public issues does not limit implementation to simply understanding how agencies organize or handle personnel issues. In addition to agencies such as the FBI and the U.S. Marshals Service (both federal agencies, for illustrative purposes only), the Congress, the courts, and even special interest groups become involved in implementation. To the extent that Congress offers specifics in legislation, it is in effect stating how a policy is to be implemented. Congressional committees also hold oversight hearings on agency activities to maintain some check on agency actions (the Waco and the Ruby Ridge incidents are examples). The courts in reviewing criminal rights and procedures in essence are determining the rules of conduct for law enforcement officials. Special interests become involved in the implementation of crime policy, for example, by cooperative efforts between law enforcement and neighborhood watch groups.

Implementation observed in the context of outcomes reveals that the contemporary liberal versus conservative debate makes it difficult to separate the technical aspects of administration from politics. For instance, in states where tougher sentencing is popular, it is potentially easier to implement "get tough" policies (Lester and Stewart, 1996). It is clear that with so many different policy actors interested and involved in policy implementation, numerous opportunities exist for politics to influence the process, outputs, and outcomes of programs. In the ideal world of public administration, implementation would be the purview of experts and managers, and not involve politics. (For example, Woodrow Wilson, when pioneering public administration in the United States, argued that administration and politics ought to remain separate; Stillman, 1996).

In today's political setting, there is little faith in government generally. The average citizen sees politics everywhere in government, not just residing with elected officials. To a certain extent, the criticism is justified. After all, if the public expects agencies to behave as political beings rather than as professionals, should we be surprised that policies enacted by Congress are more reflective of political concerns rather than solutions to problems? The failure of government to implement policy becomes a self-fulfilling prophecy.

Thus, administration is viewed with a great deal of political skepticism. From the public's perspective, programs do not work, bureaucrats are politically motivated, and agencies are power hungry. It is difficult to effectively implement policy, no matter how well developed and organized the agency may be, given today's negative political climate. A major goal of implementation is compliance. But an organization can only do so much to bring about compliance if laws are poorly crafted, the public distrusts all levels of government, and there is no consensus in society as to the goals and objectives of the policy (Mazmanian and Sabatier, 1983).

Crime policy is a perfect example of the political obstacles facing implementers. Crime policy, as we shall see in more detail in Chapter 4, is a mixed bag of liberal prevention and conservative deterrence programs. The public sends mixed signals to all levels of government. On the one hand, there is pressure to be tough on crime. On the other hand, the public becomes outraged when law enforcement attempts to crack down on the "wrong" people. It seems as if the public expects law enforcement officials to be both ruthless enforcers and caring protectors at the same time. Often, for crime agency personnel, doing one's job can become an implementation nightmare, for every action taken is potentially both the right and wrong decision.

Implementation is probably the most overlooked aspect of the policy process by decision makers. Most legislators assume that since agencies are staffed with experts in the field, implementation will take care of itself. If something goes wrong, the blame be all too quickly can be assigned to a lack of quality personnel or, less often, a badly written law. But some scholars do not overlook implementation; in this body of literature, studies on the processes, outputs, and outcomes of policy are extensive.

Studies of implementation reveal that there are many variables influencing the implementation process. Some of the more common problems include: poorly defined goals and objectives, problems of federalism, conflicting political ideologies, lack of public consensus towards a problem, and failure to identify what variables are most likely to influence implementation and under what circumstances (Ingram, 1987). (For one example of the complexities of implementation, *see* Mazmanian and Sabatier, 1983; for other approaches, *see* Goggin et al., 1990, Van Meter and Van Horn, 1975, and the pioneering work on implementation by Pressman and Wildavsky, 1973.)

Implementation problems associated with crime policy illustrate these factors quite nicely. For example, the primary goal of crime policy is to reduce crime. Unfortunately, there is no general agreement as to what the root causes of crime are—economic, social, cultural, psychological, or physical.

Additionally, there is disagreement over what is a crime. Should crimes be limited to activities against property and persons, or should "victimless" crimes such as drunkenness, drug addiction, obscenity, and prostitution be considered. In addition, we must consider environmental crime and political crime. Until these questions can be clearly answered, it is difficult to study implementation of crime policy from an outcomes perspective. Finally, as pointed out earlier, deep ideological divisions over liberal versus conservative philosophy towards crime are readily apparent throughout the policy cycle. This schism works to produce a disjointed and inconsistent environment in which crime bureaucrats are expected to function.

It is important to expose failures in implementation, but it is vital that decision makers and the public understand that the burden of proof should not be placed solely on the backs of law enforcement, corrections, or crime prevention agencies, whether national, state, or local. Failure of crime policy is not simply due to a police officer not doing his or her job, or a criminal "getting off" due to a procedural loophole. Clearly, other factors are at work: inadequate funding, understaffing, poorly written legislation, and the intractability of the problem. The failure to implement a sound crime policy is traceable to every step of the policy process, leading us to conclude that policy formulators must look both forward and backward at the same time. Every step of the policy process is important, including the feedback stage of the policy cycle to which we now turn.

POLICY EVALUATION, IMPACT, AND REVISION

There are many technical methods for evaluating policies generally, ranging from upfront approaches such as Planning Programming and Budgeting Systems (PPBS) and Cost Benefit Analysis, to sophisticated research projects designed to determine whether the program or policy is having an impact on the target audience. Broader models of evaluations include process models, where the focus is on how a program is delivered. A basic question to be answered in a process evaluation is: Did the policy reach the intended public, client, or constituent?

Developing a more efficient delivery method is often the focus of a process evaluation. Impact evaluations are concerned with whether the goals and objectives of the policy are met. Policy evaluation generally attempts to examine the impact policies have on the problem at hand. A basic question in policy analysis is—has the problem been reduced through the implementation of programs designed to address the issue?

To evaluate a policy, three basic steps must be followed in order: measurement, analysis, and recommendations. First, the problem being addressed must be measured. A baseline for comparison of before and after the policy needs to be determined. Second, an analysis needs to be conducted that compares the before and after measurements of the problem. The analysis reveals the impact (both positive and negative) the policy has had on the problem. Third, based on the analysis of the problem, recommendations are made regarding what worked, what did not work, and what to do about those aspects of the policy that failed to achieve stated policy goals and objectives. The functional activities of measurement, analysis, and recommendations produce feedback, provide information on what has changed, and measure the impact of the policy (Anderson, 1997).

The end result of policy evaluation is to provide justification for government's activities, assess the degree of change resulting from the policy, and propose alterations to be presented to decision makers as new agenda items. Thus, policy evaluation is a vital ingredient, or the fuel, that moves policy full circle. From policy evaluations, decision makers develop an arsenal of information from which proposals are fashioned to maintain, alter, scrap, or push for entirely new policies. The process of policy evaluation is both scientific and political. It is a process where objective measures and methods are imposed on a subjective political setting. Political and social research produces few, if any, hard scientific facts, which leaves the results of policy evaluation open to broad interpretation. While the need for policy evaluation is sincere and well intentioned, applying scientific research designs for the purpose of finding indisputable answers is problematic. The goals of policy evaluation are not always the same for all policy participants. For instance, agencies may overly emphasize competence and efficiency of delivery, while the public may be more concerned with the speed of delivery and whether the policy achieved results (see Figure 3.2).

We examine these two aspects of policy evaluation separately. First, basic scientific research designs are summarized to highlight the process of evaluation. Second, the problems associated with applying scientific methods to political and social issues are examined. In the end, decision makers need to determine whether some information, even if biased, is better than none.

Bureaucrat's View of Program's Success	Public's View of Program's Success
Competence ————————➤ *Responsiveness*	
(Performs job carefully)	(Respond quickly)
(Attention to detail)	(Simplify procedures)
(Well thought out)	(Deal with special circumstance)
(Well developed)	("Did I get what I wanted")
Efficiency ————————➤ *Effectiveness*	
(Routine followed)	(Respond to special cases)
(Pigeonholing of cases)	(Adjust to changing case-types)
(Few unexpected events)	(Handle unexpected events)

*The public measures success of programs on the basis of responsiveness and effectiveness. The bureaucrat needs to be aware of this, and realize competency and efficiency do not guarantee a happy public. In fact, public perception of performance may likely hinge on the handling of the unexpected, rather than the routine.

Figure 3.2.   Policy Evaluation—Program Success or Failure.
Source: Adapted from Clarence N. Stone, Robert K. Whelan, and William J. Murin, *Urban Policy and Politics in a Bureaucratic Age* (Upper Saddle River, NJ: Prentice Hall, 1986)

POLICY ANALYSIS AND EVALUATION PROCESS

Policy analysis can be separated from program evaluation. Program evaluations are typically narrow in scope, addressing primarily the benefits and costs of implementation. Usually conducted by agencies, program evaluation techniques include approaches such as cost benefit analysis (CBA), Planning Programming and Budgeting Systems (PPBS), and Management by Objectives (MBO). Program evaluations are designed to provide baseline information on agency performance (examined more closely in Chapter 6).

Policy, on the other hand, is comprehensive in nature and encompasses cause-and-effect relationships, outcomes, and impacts of policy. Policy analysis also examines and weighs alternatives for achieving goals and objectives and is not confined to simply evaluating what is current policy. Measurement, analysis, and recommendation activities of policy analysis are incorporated into a number of research design options. The most commonly used research designs include experimental research designs, pre-program post-program models, quasi-experimental designs, process analysis, and impact analysis.

Regardless of the model of choice, a primary goal of policy analysis is to determine the impact the policy is having on an issue or problem. Impacts can

be direct-intended, direct-unintended, indirect, or as a positive or negative externality—as shown in the examples below.

In crime policy, direct impacts include measurable changes in crime rates
and conviction rates. An example of an unintended consequence might be
where high technology security systems produce a reduction in burglaries, resulting in fewer arrests, which should not be confused with law enforcement
officials being lax in the performance of their duties. A reduction in the crime
rate followed by an increase in economic growth in a community might be
viewed as an externality. A spin-off effect of the growth of high technology
communications could be the ability of the criminal to more easily trace the
movement of police (or vice versa).

It may be useful to compare analytical research designs applied to crime issues. Experimental designs establish a control group and an experimental
group to study the differences or changes that occur by introducing a new policy, program, or law into a defined population and comparing the results with
a group where the program is not present. For instance, an analyst could compare similar communities where Neighborhood Watch groups exist (experimental group) with an area where there is no community program of this type.
Differences in reported crimes, disturbances, and arrests could be measured
and compared in analyzing the utility of this type of citizen policing mechanism. As one can probably guess, there are many hurdles to this type of study.
Where does a researcher find two "similar" communities? How does one control for factors other than the watch group as influences on neighborhood
safety? Experimental designs must be carefully constructed or the results
quickly can become spurious.

Preprogram and post-program studies are even less scientific than experimental designs. Many are simply case studies where the analyst observes over
time the changes that take place in a community before and after a policy is
implemented. For instance, the researcher might study incidents of gun-re-
lated crimes comparing rates before and after the implementation of a waiting period on the purchase of firearms. Perhaps the most serious limitation of
this type of study is its inability to take into account alternative explanations
for changes in crime rates.

Quasi-experimental designs seek to compare and contrast a number of existing programs at a time. They have the advantage of increasing the number of
points of study and provide a greater ability to study a wider variety of cause-
and-effect relationships. This type of study is severely limited, however, in that
it becomes extremely difficult to control for the absence of any single variable.
Quasi-experimental designs are less scientific than experimental designs, but
because of their broad scope, can be politically more acceptable to decision
makers who want to see issues from a "big picture" perspective.

Process analysis attempts to single out the role of administration and management on policy success or failure. Such studies will explore organizational, personnel, and procedural influences on policy. The goal is to improve the implementation process and to make sure that bureaucracy does not get in the way of policy performance. It is an analytical approach in that process studies seek to improve policy by improving the performance of government generally.

In many respects, this text sets up a type of process analysis device by providing the researcher with a roadmap to better understanding of policy through the policy cycle. The goal is not only to better understand crime policy but also to better understand how the system works, thus enhancing the opportunity to improve policy. Process analysis is limiting in that its focus on government can minimize the role of social, cultural, and economic factors that influence crime. However, seen from a systems perspective, process analysis can be criticized as being so broad that everything can be exposed as a cause of crime with very little guidance as to which causes are the most important to address.

Impact analysis is a five-step process: (1) the issue under investigation is operationalized, (2) goals and objectives of the policy addressing the issue are observed in operation, (3) causality is assigned based on observations, (4) a framework is developed and implemented assessing the impact of the policy, and (5) findings are reported. The step-by-step approach is scientific in technique and provides clear guidelines for conducting research. A primary drawback to impact analysis is that social issues are extremely difficult to operationalize. Researchers commonly disagree over what to measure, how to measure, and even whether the problem is something that can be quantified. In crime policy, for instance, there are numerous ways of calculating crime rates ranging from reported crime to estimates of crime. An impact analysis will produce varying results depending on how the term *crime rate* is operationalized.

PROBLEMS OF POLICY EVALUATION AND REVISION

Upon completion of the feedback stage, decision makers undertake the task of determining whether to preserve, alter, or scrap a policy. Complete elimination of a program or policy is rare for several reasons. First, social issues are ongoing and seldom if ever completely eradicated. Thus, they require routine attention. Second, since the policy process is a product of politics, the requirements of compromise and consensus produce incremental changes at best (Lindblom, 1959). Third, social issues are difficult to study scientifically.

Scientific studies of issues such as crime are flawed because cause and effects of most issues are difficult to accurately identify, let alone measure.

The process of policy analysis indicates that issues such as crime do not lend themselves neatly to the methods and techniques of scientific research. Yet, these techniques are the best we currently have to offer in the field of analysis. The demand remains high for quantity and quality information. As long as this is the case, analysis will continue, albeit incomplete analysis. Without firm answers as to which way to proceed, variations of current policies appear to be more politically, and to some degree analytically, wise than sweeping reform.

No matter how well intended, policy analysis and evaluation is conducted by people with biases. Already we have noted that program evaluations performed by agencies have a built-in bias towards protecting the work of agencies. In addition, since policies are often vague and poorly developed, people do not uniformly agree on the causes of a problem such as crime.

It is difficult for policy analysts and policymakers to assess, analyze, and make recommendations on how to deal with issues and improve policies when there is so much disagreement over defining the problem. As we shall see in Chapter 4, when the Clinton crime bill and the Republican alternative are dissected, data can be interpreted to mean just about anything and to justify almost any policy proposal.

Policy revision is incremental. The lengthy policy process combined with politics make sweeping change difficult, short of a crisis situation. Even then, the pressure to do something leads decision makers to analogous solutions to problems, and then evidence rarely leads policymakers to new paths of action. Creativity is rare. When a crisis occurs, whether real or perceived, it does not follow that genius or invention will occur like magic to solve the problem. Crime is an old problem that is traditionally dealt with through old remedies packaged as new ideas. Policy revision is designed to correct errors with the promise that exposing errors will slowly work to improve policy over time.

SUMMARY

The policy cycle reveals the complexities of how government works. This in its own right makes understanding the policy cycle important to becoming an effective participant in government and policy making. For students of criminal justice, understanding the policy cycle is the first step to becoming involved in all aspects of government decision making. It is vital that criminal justice students and practitioners realize that their interests are more than implementation of a program. The work of students and practitioners is affected every day by activities associated with agenda setting, policy formation, policy adoption, policy evaluation, and policy revision, in addition to policy implementation. Thus, understanding the policy cycle is the first step towards becoming a more informed and effective participant and practitioner in the crime policy arena.

REVIEW QUESTIONS

1. What are the benefits and limitations of the policy cycle approach to analyzing issues?
2. What are the keys to successfully getting an issue on the agenda?
3. With respect to policy formation, what factors need to be considered in developing or proposing a viable option?
4. Discuss how the Congress, the president, and the courts are involved in making crime policy?
5. What factors can influence the implementation process?
6. What are the advantages/disadvantages of policy analysis frameworks?

Chapter Four

The Policy Cycle Applied
to the Crime Issue

LEARNING OBJECTIVES

In this chapter, you will do the following:

1. Discover how the policy-cycle framework can be applied to crime to gain a more analytical perspective of the issue
2. Assess the 2001 USA Patriot Act
3. Distinguish between politics, process, and policy in current efforts to deal with the crime issue
4. Learn the basic components of producing a "better" bill
5. Evaluate the utility of the policy cycle as a means of studying terrorism

INTRODUCTION

For the policy cycle to be a practical analytical technique, it needs to be applied to real issues and problems. All too often, policy texts put forth a policy cycle for students to use when examining policies, but they never fully incorporate the model into an analysis of issues (*see* Anderson, 1997, for example). Many policy texts include the various stages and steps of the policy cycle but leave application to others. There are a few texts (Lester and Stewart, 1996, for example) that provide a variation of the policy cycle followed by several exploring current issues. However, in every instance the discussions on issues are merely an overview of the topic and offer no organized effort to incorporate the policy cycle into the discussion. The reader is left to fill in the gaps and speculate on whether the issue is a reflection of agenda setting, policy formation, government action, implementation, evaluation, or revision. In contrast, in this chapter current legislation is analyzed from a step-by-step, policy-cycle approach. The reader is given the opportunity to directly apply the policy cycle to a contemporary issue, namely crime.

The focus of this chapter is on how politics and process work to cloud fact and apply fiction with respect to the crime issue. The policy-cycle framework applied to crime policy reveals that the 2001 USA Patriot Act is woefully inadequate as a response to address domestic terrorism or as an aid to combat global terrorism. Further, as the chapter progresses, whether in agenda setting or policy evaluation, it becomes clear that the root causes of terrorism are not directly addressed. Instead, Republican and Democratic proposals reflect philosophical and constituency concerns and perspectives.

Both Democratic and Republican approaches to terrorism have been incomplete, deferential to the President, and inconsistent with the tradition of civil liberties. Passage and subsequent discussion of the Patriot Act was perfunctory, and there is little evidence that the politics both sides engaged in are intentionally designed to seriously address terrorism.

Part of the disjoint between terrorism and our response arises mostly from ideology. The scholarly literature relating to terrorism is somewhat incomplete, and while the extensive data ought to lead to some coherent solutions, more research seems to add to the confusion of legislators. As more information is gathered, the marketplace of ideas and solutions relating to terrorism become increasingly cluttered. Additionally, with the volumes of data, there are greater opportunities for policy advocates to pick and choose only the "facts" that reinforce preexisting philosophical views, ideological perspectives, and constituency concerns regarding terrorism.

The Department of Homeland Security, created shortly after the terror attack of September 11, 2001, has done very little to protect the homeland. It has become a haven for cronies and pork projects, as reported in outlets such as the Washington Post, New York Times and government reports, with very little of its work being aimed at detecting and apprehending terrorists. The policy cycle reveals that political expediency and pressure to do something with respect to terrorism created these conditions, and our policy against domestic terrorism and violence are not well-developed based on reasoning or analytical objectivity.

The consequences of applying the policy cycle process to the Patriot Act are significant for criminal justice students and practitioners. The policy cycle reveals that government's efforts to address the crime issue, for the most part, result in policies that send mixed signals to all concerned. The public sees a policy that attempts to do a great deal but accomplishes very little. Ideological constituencies continue to be dissatisfied because their unique perspectives are never fully adopted into policy. Experts continue to be frustrated because the evidence is never fully embraced by decision makers. Criminal justice students and practitioners are confused by laws that expect agencies to be tougher on terrorism, but require strict adherence to the protection of individual rights. We now turn to developing these perspectives as revealed through the lens of the policy cycle.

POLICY INPUTS

Terrorism perpetrated on the soil of the United States is rare. Prior to the September 11, 2001, the only domestic terror attack attributable to foreign terrorists was the 1995 World Trade Center bombing. Terrorism is not new to the United States, however. Domestic terrorism has been conducted against organized labor, racial minorities, and ethnic groups. Machine politics of urban areas has led some citizens to live in fear of their own government. Organized crime has undermined the social fabric of society including government. While previous domestic terrorism was treated as general crime issue, a concerted effort against eliminating terrorism did not occur until the United States suffered attacks on its economic and military centers of power by a foreign source. There are several decent explanations for this inattention to terrorism.

The end of the Cold War has allowed national political figures to focus almost entirely on domestic issues. The Clinton campaign and presidency were unique in that the policy focus was overwhelmingly domestic in nature (*see* Jones, 1996; Quirk and Hinchcliffe, 1996; and Berman and Goldman, 1996). This is not to suggest that until the end of the Cold War citizens did not worry about crime; *see,* for example, President Johnson's Commission on Law Enforcement and the Administration of Justice. The point is, it was not until the end of the Cold War that Washington was pushed to focus on domestic issues such as crime, which heretofore had primarily a state and local concern. This political environment serves as the backdrop for agenda setting and the formation of current national crime policy.

September 11, 2001 provided the political wind to do something about terrorism. Horrific images from New York, Pennsylvania, and Washington were played along with the tattered, scared voices of those who died in the crashed planes. Family members who lost loved ones showed pictures of family and recounted the last words they spoke to those they deeply cared about. Nationally, the United States was paralyzed in the aftermath of the attacks. All commercial flights were grounded, Wall Street suspended trading, and President Bush burrowed deeply into a fortified bunker to devise a strategy to go after the villains responsible.

AGENDA SETTING

Ball (2004) asserts that the USA Patriot Act was the culmination of a series of events over the span of years beginning with the 1983 U.S. embassy bombing in Beirut, Lebanon. Contemporary acts of aggression against the United States included the bombing of the World Trade Center in 1995 only twelve years after the Beirut bombing, and those bombings that targeted U.S. embassies in Africa and the U.S.S. Cole in 1998 and 2000, respectively. As mentioned earlier, domestic terrorism was nothing new for the United States when September 11, 2001 occurred. The most recent manifestation was evident in the work of the Olympic bomber Eric Rudolph and the Oklahoma City bomber Timothy McVeigh. Foreign-spawned terrorism, until September 11, largely had been carried out on the international stage. Thus, the policymakers and law enforcement officials had been dealing with terrorism for quite some time, but with very little success.

Historically, conservatives had resisted expanding law enforcement powers that would allow police and intelligence functions to circumvent civil liberties and directly address the limitations placed on law enforcement. In a twist of irony, U.S. Attorney General John Ashcroft in his former role as Senator from Missouri criticized a Clinton Administration proposal that would have given law enforcement officers some of the same powers as the USA Patriot Act permitted. His criticism of the proposal centered on resisting giving more power to what he called the "jack booted thugs" of law enforcement. His sentiments were shared by others, and the resistance to expanded law enforcement authority was successful. Many citizens could rightly ask, what changed?

The 9/11 terror attacks happened on the watch of a conservative President. Much of his cabinet shared a similar ideology. The neo-conservative movement has a foremost thirst for strong wielding of power and global dominance over inferior powers, including international organizations such as the United Nations. Being victims of terrorism shocked the conscience of all U.S. citizens and their leaders. Civil liberties thus took a backseat to the exercise of power. Government went about claiming for itself those tools necessary to gather more information about potential terrorist activities, and geared up for a massive military operation. Patriot Act provisions became the domestic tools, since the terrorist were living in the United States and received much of their flight training here, too.

The Patriot Act came along at the right time. In this regard, it is like most other justice policies. In a time of crisis, policymakers may use good will, cooperation, and a rallying-around-the-flag effect to accomplish policy goals that otherwise may be unattainable. Patriot Act provisions were easily placed on the agenda due to the panic that occurred after the 9/11 terror attack, and the frustrations of ineffectively dealing with terrorism over a forty year period. Most importantly, the catastrophic events of 9/11 did more to nudge the policy agenda to respond to terrorism, but the events did not provide the impetus for any carefully crafted response to domestic terrorist threats. Most law enforcement officers, if honest, will admit they are only marginally more prepared to combat terrorism and be first responders than when the 9/11 attacks occurred.

POLICY FORMATION

The current rhetoric regarding the Patriot Act suggests that the contents of the bill and its implementation are forays into undiscovered territory. Careful examination of the 2001 Patriot Act reveals that the contents of the act are a law enforcer's wish list. Since the Warren Court era, law enforcement has viewed the courts as hostile to their work. Thus, we can view the relationship between our crime fighting agencies and the courts as a tenuous one. This tenuous relationship has formed the foundation for the leap towards lessening the restrictions on government and its ability to gather evidence and prosecute crime.

During the Warren Court era, the Supreme Court incorporated much of the Bill of Rights upon the states. Nationalization of the Bill of Rights began roughly in the 1930s with cases dealing with the right to an attorney. The most notable case is *Powell v. Alabama* (1932), which is also known as the Scottsboro Boys' case. Nine black males were accused of raping two white women while all of them were hitching a ride on a freight train. Without the availability of an attorney, the accused were convicted and sentenced to death. In this case, the Supreme Court held that the Constitution does grant due process, and in this case it had been violated. This began a series of cases involving the expansion of civil liberties and rights of the accused.

Some of the notable cases decided during the Warren Era include *Miranda v. Arizona*, *Gideon v. Wainwright*, and *Mapp v. Ohio*. In addition to the rapid expansion of the rights of the accused, the Warren Court also upheld and forced other federal courts to enforce the Civil Rights Act of 1964, the Voting Rights Act 1965, and the Fair Housing Act 1968. These cases routinely sided with citizens who had been disfranchised by government power and abuses. Subsequent decisions by the federal courts have expanded civil rights to include prohibitions on sexual harassment while upholding controversial policies such as affirmative action.

Contemporary political struggles over the judiciary revolve around whether the courts have expanded civil rights and liberties too far (Rothwax,

1996). Most recently, the War on Terrorism has spawned new controversies revolving around the USA Patriot Act and how to balance liberty and security. Under provisions of the Patriot Act, government's authority has been substantially increased. Investigatory authority of federal, state, and local police agencies has been expanded to include broadened sneak and peak search authority (searches conducted without prior notice and in the absence of the suspect) and enhanced power for prosecutors (Schmalleger, 2005). This act further increases the ability of federal authorities to tap phones (including wireless devices) and track Internet usage. In essence, the Patriot Act permits law enforcement to engage in activities that many consider a violation of the civil liberties embodied in the Constitution.

Many critics of the Patriot Act contend that then Attorney General John Ashcroft had the desire to implement many of its provisions, but could only do so if a national tragedy such as horrific terrorist attacks occurred. In fact, the Patriot Act was proposed hastily and in a matter of days after the attacks on the Pentagon and the World Trade Center. Much of the proposal did not represent a careful examination of the failures and deficiencies of the law enforcement and intelligence agencies that led to the attacks. Rather, it was a collection of old policies that were taken off the shelf and dressed up as the new powers they needed to combat terrorism (Center for National Security Studies, 2005).

Thus, the Patriot Act is a prime example of policy formation that does not easily fit into most policy models. However, our model neatly allows for a step-by-step comparison of those involved in the policy formation. As mentioned previously, some (including us) view policy as controlled by elite interests. The Patriot Act was proposed by Attorney General Ashcroft and he requested that no modifications be made unless legislators wanted to run the risk of another terror attack. Other key players in the development included the respective Judiciary Committee Chairs in the House of Representatives and the Senate.

By engaging in the conflict and compromise that arises when liberals such as Patrick Leahy (D-VT and Senate Judiciary Chairman) and conservatives such as James Sensenbrenner (R-WI and House Judiciary Chairperson), the Patriot Act could normatively be thought of as reflecting the entire ideological spectrum. We are not convinced the Act does represent such a cross section. On some policy issues such as terrorism, the government's response may transcend traditional ideological boundaries. We believe the Patriot Act is such a piece of crime fighting policy. Make no mistake, controversy abounds and we will discuss that aspect in the evaluation section. For now, it is important to note that the Patriot Act was formulated in response to a crisis. Yet, the integral components responsible for developing the proposals—elites— remain a constant aspect of the policy process.

Examining the policy formation stage of the policy cycle reveals a eerily pragmatic, or trial and error approach, to developing public policy. The symbolism of the Patriot Act and the lack of any comprehensive alternative suggest that government has a haphazard approach towards fighting terrorism, and, in reality, each deals with only small aspects of the problem. Gaps in policy are numerous, but can be summed up in government's inability to find the political and material resources to deal with terrorism in its entirety and complexity.

GOVERNMENT ACTION

The decision-making process with respect to the Patriot Act can be examined in three steps. First, we examine the bill from the perspective of efforts to build and mobilize political support. Second, we review the actual legislative decision-making process and action taken on each the bill to reveal the methods of reaching a consensus on the issue. Third, we make an assessment of congressional action on crime policy based on the analysis of the first two steps; namely, the mobilization of support and the decision-making process.

MOBILIZATION OF POLITICAL SUPPORT

Political scientists have used foreign crises as a variable that explains support for the President and government in general (Erikson and Tedin, 2002). This "rally-around-the-flag" effect gives politicians a good bit of currency that can be used to mobilize support for otherwise controversial measures. Since many of the Patriot Act provisions were, and remain controversial, proponents of its provisions have regularly reminded the public that the United States is under the threat of attack.

Law enforcement groups, including the national police organizations, have found themselves in favor of the Patriot Act. Leaders view terrorism as an issue that concerns citizens and some important core constituencies. Civil libertarians and groups such as the American Library Association have banded together to resist many of the provisions of the Patriot Act. They have largely been unsuccessful. Since several of the Patriot Act provisions were sunset provisions, many of the initial opponents of the Act have girded to fight the renewal. On this matter they have been successful. We will look at that a bit later.

Interest groups in the United States exhibit a great deal of diversity and range from individuals to large organizations that are well funded. Their job is to attempt to persuade government officials (both elected and unelected) about public problems, opportunities, and policy options (Lindblom and

Woodhouse, 1993). In spite of a traditional distaste for interest groups, they play an important part in the policy process: (1) they clarify and articulate what citizens want, (2) they help sort out an impossible number of policy options and overcome conflict of interests, (3) they monitor governance, (4) they serve as an important source of information, and (5) they help in building working coalitions to pass pending legislation (Lindblom and Woodhouse, 1993).

Increasingly, these groups are asked to testify and provide position papers to congressional committees and subcommittees. In the matter of the Patriot Act, external influence is minimal. The Patriot Act can be viewed as being influenced by a select few bureaucratic agencies, such as the FBI, and the power of public opinion for Congress to do something to keep America safe.

THE DECISION MAKING PROCESS

Congressional action on the Patriot Act was largely uncontested. The mix of liberal ideology and conservative get-tough provisions did not provide the impetus for much conflict. Not much compromise was needed as both parties wanted to be seen as protecting American citizens. However, divisions within the parties did exist, but the rank and file in each party disciplined themselves to remove the politics during a time when the United States was in shock. This environment clouded many of the post 9/11 policies, not just the Patriot Act.

Members of Congress viewed future struggles over the Patriot Act as where the hard battles would be fought. In fact, within a couple of years, some members of Congress had proposed amendments to the Patriot Act related to tracking Internet activity and obtaining medical, financial, and library records. The conduct of the war on terror did not help quell the suspicions of staunch civil libertarians, even though some of the provisions—library record scans—had not been used within the first year. Ultimately, the decision-making process guiding the Patriot Act showed virtual unanimity to project solidarity.

ASSESSMENT OF CONGRESSIONAL
ACTION ON TERRORISM

The September 11th Commission found that the United States had a lack of imagination in tackling the problem of terrorism. Both Republican and Democratic administrations have failed to adequately address terrorism, while some believe the only way is through the use of force. (Cheney, 2005). Terrorism policy had been ad hoc and reactionary to specific events with very few comprehensive solutions. This strategy has produced disjointed pieces of legislation that appeared to be more of a craving for political junk food and beltway candy rather than a healthy balanced diet of pragmatic solutions.

Studying congressional decision making reveals that policy is more about how to pass a law than whether the law is any good. Analysis of government action on terrorism also confirms the incremental nature of the congressional process (Lindblom, 1959). Further, the government action stage of the policy cycle reveals that there are many ways to define what is "good" terrorism policy, most of them politically, not scientifically, based. Policy produced in this manner has major implications for implementation. The general consequences of policymaking on implementation are examined below. Specific effects of the policymaking process and techniques for implementing policy wrapped in politics are explored in Part Three (Chapters 5 to 7) of this text.

POLICY OUTPUTS: WAGING WAR ON TERROR

The Patriot Act has been implemented with mixed success. Thus, assessing implementation efforts is limited to projecting what problems and benefits are associated with it. However, Congress often passes laws that are vague and unclear (Edwards and Wayne, 2005). In addition, Congress often passes laws that have inconsistent goals, and the laws rarely include steps necessary to put a program into effect (Gordon and Milokovich, 1995). This means that bureaucrats must interpret the language and make a guess as to the intent of the formulators.

The result is, as Marion (1995) points out, that bureaucrats have a good deal of power in policy implementation in terms of creating policy details, having information about the specifics of the problem(s), and enforcing regulations. When bureaucrats move policy in an ideological direction inconsistent with the policy desires of Congress, however, legislative backlash can occur. Mass opinion also can change, which further inflames policymakers. Such is the case with the Patriot Act.

What we have seen while implementing the Patriot Act has been a trampling of civil liberties, both for "enemy combatants" and U.S. citizens suspected of terrorist activities. Suspects have been held without notification of charges or access to an attorney, and some are targeted without probable cause. In a 2003, the Justice Department Inspector General released a report detailing dozens of incidents where Patriot Act provisions were abused, including the detaining of Muslims for immigration violations and the targeting of Muslims in general.

Shortly after the Patriot Act passed, the Justice Department also targeted a round up of Arabs in the town of Dearborn, Michigan (the largest concentration of Middle Easterners in the United States). Observers of the policy speculated that the only basis for their targeting was their ethnic and religious backgrounds. No prior information would have led the Justice Department to conclude that the Dearborn residents had any law enforcement value or knowledge of terrorist activities.

Provisions of the Patriot Act have also been used, along with Executive Order, to deprive those detained as suspected terrorists of legal representation and due process. For almost three years after September 11, 2001, the Bush administration pushed policies that sought to limit the Constitutional protections of terrorist suspects. The Supreme Court rejected these measures in *Hamdi et al v. Rumsfeld* . Justice O' Connor, speaking for the majority asserted "(w)e have long since made clear that a state of war is not a blank check for the President when it comes to the rights of the nation's citizens (*Hamdi et al v. Rumsfeld*, 2004)."

There have also been reports that suspects in U.S. custody have been abused by agents and military personnel. The most noted case involved the Iraqi prison Abu Grahib. Prisoners there were beaten, humiliated, and some were killed. Photographs of their naked bodies were shown on the Internet and the evening news. During the investigation of the reports, similar stories began to emerge from other facilities where suspects were being held. Shortly after the passage of the Patriot Act, government lawyers led by White House Counsel Alberto Gonzales began to relax rules related to the treatment of prisoners including torture policies.

Implementation of the Patriot Act, and subsequent extensions regarding the custody of suspects, has a checkered past. Many of the abuses of prisoners, and violations of civil liberties, were sanctioned and encouraged by the President. Several years after the passage of the Patriot Act, we are still learning about its implementation and drift that has occurred while carrying out the response to terrorism. We would suggest that the implementation of the Patriot Act runs contrary to the spirit of the Constitution and limits on government. The Patriot Act renewal did not include curbs sought by advocates of personal freedom from government interference.

FEEDBACK

The final stage of the policy cycle centers on evaluation and revision of policy to reflect findings resulting from the measurement and analysis of policy. It is too early to fully assess national policy efforts, but the recent past is not positive. Thus, the focus here will be on summarizing the general measurable evidence relating to fighting terrorism. From this overview of the data regarding crime, we offer a preliminary assessment of current national efforts in crime policy. Finally, we present a list of recommendations for improving the federal government's policy towards fighting terrorism.

POLICY EVALUATION

If the goal of the Patriot Act is to prevent terrorist attacks on United States soil by giving law enforcement the tools necessary to gather evidence and prosecute cases, then the Patriot Act has been successful. Terrorism, however, has increased significantly since the terror attacks of September 11, 2001. While the United States has not had a terror attack on any domestic targets, devastating terrorist attacks have occurred all over the globe. Most experts, and regular citizens, believe the United States is not safer now than when the terrorist attacks of 2001 occurred. These conclusions are drawn from government assessments, public statements by government officials, and public opinion polling. Government agencies such as the Government Accountability Office and Inspectors General frequently publish findings that demonstrate gaps in port security, mass transit security, and critical infrastructure. What then can explain this paradox?

Many of the Patriot Acts' provisions are unknown to most citizens. Therefore, when the Justice Department uses some of the power available to it, citizens are not aware of that work. John Ashcroft, as he was leaving his post as Attorney General, noted that one of his mistakes as attorney general was not fully explaining the Patriot Act to the American public. In essence, he believed strongly in the Patriot Act and the successes in law enforcement that it led to, but in his mind he did not properly communicate those successes.

While government may not have found its voice in promoting the Patriot Act, opponents have railed against it since its inception. Not surprisingly, many of the opponents of the Patriot Act come from across the ideological spectrum. Both liberal and staunch conservatives have shared a commonality: government cannot be trusted with much power. Liberal and conservative groups fear that the Patriot Act allows government agents to trample civil liberties, and sets up the government as the biggest threat to individual freedom—not the terrorists as political leaders assert.

In leading the way on fighting terrorism, President Bush has hailed the Patriot Act as an integral part of the war on terrorism. In a speech on June 9, 2005, President Bush asserted:

> Over the past three-and-a-half years, America's law enforcement and intelligence personnel have proved that the Patriot Act works, that it was an important piece of legislation. Since September the 11th, federal terrorism investigations

have resulted in charges against more than 400 suspects, and more than half of those charged have been convicted. Federal, state, and local law enforcement have used the Patriot Act to break up terror cells in New York and Oregon and Virginia and in Florida. We've prosecuted terrorist operatives and supporters in California, in Texas, in New Jersey, in Illinois, and North Carolina and Ohio. These efforts have not always made the headlines, but They've made communities safer. The Patriot Act has accomplished exactly what it was designed to do — it has protected American liberty, and saved American lives (White House, June 9, 2005).

Opponents do not share his optimism, and point out these successes are not integral for fighting terrorism when weighed against the threats to civil liberties. They would highlight the cases where law enforcement has detained citizens without probable cause, treated them less than humanely while in custody, and denied them due process guaranteed by the Constitution.

POLICY REVISION

Policy, as with most issues, is the product of politics and analysis. These two forces, one subjective and the other objective, define the practical limitations of policy revision. Policy revision is also about pondering the unknown and untried. Contemplating the possibility of an "ideal" justice policy assists in better understanding current policy. Further, as researchers brainstorm about alternative policy options, they gain a better appreciation as to the trials and tribulations facing decision makers who are asked to pass legislation in the real world, not in a hypothetical setting. The analysis of crime policy in the context of the policy cycle reveals at least four possible courses of action: maintain the status quo, adopt a strictly liberal strategy, follow a conservative approach, or undertake a comprehensive policy approach. We briefly examine the prospects and limitations of each option below. We argue that the most likely course of action will be to maintain the status quo. We discuss the circumstances necessary to produce a comprehensive and effective crime policy as well as the political, constitutional, economic, and social costs of a more "serious" approach to terror threats.

MAINTAINING THE STATUS QUO

The first option, to maintain the status quo, is pragmatic both politically and scientifically. Elected decision makers are comfortable in repeating the analogous and routine. Repeating old policies brings order into what often seems to be a chaotic political environment. Decision makers may not be satisfied with specific components of a bill that for the most part reinvents the wheel, but it is an approach that is at least partially measurable both politically and scientifically. Symbolic rhetoric, such as declaring war on drugs, helps suggest new commitments and new approaches to crime are being made without having to drastically alter (increase) resources.

Preserving the status quo makes a great deal of sense if the government is unwilling to shift expenditures, dramatically increase spending, or raise taxes. Maintaining the current mix of military action along with covert law enforcement allows all sides to claim expenditure of efforts on the pressing terrorism issues while only symbolically increasing their commitment to solving the root causes of the problem. This approach also may be what the public really wants out of government regarding this issue. While public support for protecting America is at an all-time high (the elections of 2002 and 2004 attest to this fact), citizens also do not want government to raise taxes, increase the deficit, or significantly increase spending in this area at the expense of other programs. In essence, citizens expect government to do more with less, in part from the perception that government cannot be trusted and is characterized by waste, fraud, and abuse.

Preserving the status quo also diminishes the prospects of frequent and major constitutional conflicts. As it currently stands, Constitutional issues have surfaced over the implementation of the Patriot Act, defendant rights, privacy considerations, and the like. Maintaining the current policy at a minimum keeps the Constitutional debate within recognizable parameters. Public desire to balance freedom with a strong police state pushes decision makers to operate within traditional perspectives for dealing with crime. lack of a credible public consensus as to what to do about terrorism, along with conflicting goals, lead decision makers to continue the status quo.

ADOPTING A LIBERAL STRATEGY?

President Bush believes that it is important to spread democracy in the Middle East if we are going to be successful in blunting the appeal of radical Islam and terrorism. However as discussed earlier, the liberal strategy assumes that societal and economic factors cause terrorism. For liberals, the policy emphasis is on prevention. In the long term, solutions to the cause of terrorism include reducing world-wide poverty, modernizing international law, and forging stronger alliances with less developed countries. The liberal approach greatly expands the role of government and requires a huge commitment in resources to have any chance of succeeding.

The liberal approach holds promise as a remedy if individuals turn to terrorism out of frustration associated with the constraints imposed by their environment (Lester and Stewart, 1996). However, studies on the reasons for terrorism are far from conclusive. In terms of criminal activity, Wilson and Hernstein (1985), for example, contend that many criminals are rational human beings who conclude that crime does indeed pay. Thus, where criminals see crime as worth the risk, the venture is more like an individual career choice than to environmental factors or biomedical factors that point to genetic factors as causes of crime (Brennan et al., 1995). We do not have similar insights into terrorism

The question that must be answered is whether the cost of such programs outweigh the benefits? For the liberal perspective to gain in importance, government must shake its wasteful and fraudulent image. Additionally, liberals must offer convincing evidence to the public that the emphasis on social and environmental factors benefits the security of everyday Americans. In the United States, there is clearly a deep populist belief that the public can and is willing to pool its resources to tackle common problems (Dionne, 1991). To the extent that terrorism is a rallying point for public action, the liberal perspective is likely to continue to be a vital component of future policy approaches.

THE CONSERVATIVE APPROACH

In contrast to the liberal notion that societal structures and economic factors are major contributors to terrorism, the conservative approach holds that too little exertion of state power has contributed to the feeding of terrorism (Cheney, 2005). If we only apply sufficient U.S. power, we would then curb terrorist impulses, thus bringing about an end to the view that terrorism is a viable means for achieving political goals. This perspective has proven wanting with the public as the President's handling of terrorism is at all time low.

The conservative approach to terrorism also runs counter to their historic distrust of government power. Many of the solutions thus far—dismantling civil liberties, expanding the military—lack of vision, and disdain for dissent; they have produced distrust, mounting debt, and overextended the military without the corresponding benefits that the liberal approach would be subjected to. It is also worth noting that many of the conservative plans in combating terrorism have been embraced by liberals in the short term. Long-term, it appears the conservative approach is untenable.

COMPREHENSIVE APPROACH

Since both the current liberal and conservative approaches are flawed, where do we turn? Our overview of the policy cycle reveals that government works best under conditions conducive to compromise and consensus. Policy analysts also need to remember that progress typically must be measured in incremental steps. Change is not going to occur overnight. With these factors in mind, policy analysts and practitioners have an important role to play in turning justice policy away from ideology and electoral game rhetoric and towards a pragmatic and more comprehensive approach.

Policy analysis can help incorporate the best of both the left and the right into a more rational and less politically centered attack on the issue of terrorism. It is essential for policy students and practitioners to not only understand the policy cycle but also to use the strategies and tactics of effective participation so that they can become effective players in the political process rather than bystanders. All the good ideas and research efforts undertaken in the study of public problems are merely academic exercises unless the effort is made to educate elected officials, other practitioners, students, and most importantly, the public on the extensive problems and challenges ahead.

The research opportunities revealed by the policy cycle are numerous. States and communities in our federal system of government have authority to experiment with many different strategies. While states and communities provide laboratory-like conditions to study innovative strategies, most of the research is snapshot in nature. That is, like a photograph, events and actors are held in place while the scientist studies the policy, and typically it is more interesting to study something new than to replicate previous research to test its validity. In this vein, research needs to continue investigating the cause of terrorism, domestic implications for law enforcement, and sweeping policies that are not comprehensive. Only through observation over time can we begin to fully realize if politically expedient remedies will be long-term solutions. Academicians need to make their findings more understandable to the public and legislators to clear up some of the confusion about the causes of crime.

SUMMARY

Terrorism did not come to the forefront of policy concerns until the brutal attacks of September 11, 2001. Since that time, the attacks have been used to promote policies that have been subjected to very little debate. The consequences of such an approach to policy are that it leads to inadequacy. We have known for some time that policies are rarely produced that have as their basis solving problems. Rather, they are politically expedient policies meant only to convey symbolism and not substance. In the case of the Patriot Act, we have a policy that undermines civil liberties, has created severe divisions, and has the potential to threaten individual freedom. While implementing the Patriot Act provisions, we have indeed stepped upon a slippery slope. For example, detainee abuses, infringements upon due process, and abuses of power have been noted in the implementation of the Patriot Act. Despite these concerns, we do not envision grand alternations to the Patriot Act, or a lessening in the current pursuits to fight terrorism. Thus, the policy process is dominated by those we would come to expect to wield power, and by those factors such as ideology and expediency that do very little to promote utilitarian policies.

Periodically, we are reminded that the threat of a terrorist attack in the United States is a very real possibility. Terrorism is such an elusive act that experts do not think it is a matter of "if" another attack will happen, but rather a matter of when. The Patriot Act has attracted many supporters and many detractors. Most law enforcement personnel tell us that they do not feel any more empowered and prepared for fighting domestic terrorism than they did before 9/11/00. It is doubtful that we will be saddled with a permanent version of the Patriot Act, as the President has called for. Rather, we will continue to see the incremental changes in policy that have come to define the policy process.

REVIEW QUESTIONS

1. How does the policy cycle reveal mixed signals sent to the public about attempts to deal with crime?
2. Who controlled the agenda for the passing the Patriot Act?
3. Has the Patriot Act been successful?

Chapter Five

Mission Statements and Policies and Procedures

LEARNING OBJECTIVES

In this chapter, you will do the following:

1. Learn the importance of a mission statement and how to write a mission statement.
2. Compare mission statements of organizations with what you learn in this chapter.
3. Learn how to write effective policy and procedures.
4. Learn the importance of the role of the chief executive officer.

INTRODUCTION

Criminal justice organizations are human contrivances designed to preserve the peace, prosecute at trials of the accused, and supervise those persons found guilty of violation of the law. As human organizations, they are influenced by variables such as differing values, differing personal and institutional agendas, and the day-to-day problems that plague us all.

Criminal justice organizations exist within a framework consisting of the U.S. Constitution, the various state constitutions, statutes, professional and state standards, policies and procedures, job descriptions, and post orders. All are designed to provide order and legality to our actions and to assure that all citizens are accorded their individual rights. In addition, the organization operates, within limits, smoothly and with as few problems as possible.

Each organization has a defined set of goals, both informal and formal, that can work in opposition to each other. Conflicting aims can thwart the mission of the organization to the extent that neither the public nor the employees are sure of the mission of the organization. Formal goals are those goals established by the organization and its managers as desirable results of concerted action (Houston, 1995). They should be clearly stated in the organization's charter, mission statement, or in key statements by the head of the organization. Goals are also often specified in the Management by Objectives (MBO) annual statement. Clearly, there must be a statement of some kind that spells out the overall objective of the organization.

THE IMPORTANCE OF MISSION STATEMENTS

In an earlier work, Houston (1995) points out that a mission statement "provides direction in formulating goals." In addition, the mission statement is defined as "an enduring statement of purpose that distinguishes an organization from other similar enterprises" (David, 1986). Bozeman and Phatak (1989) define a mission statement as the purpose society expects of the organization and its responsibilities as an organization. Dupree (1990) views a mission statement as a "broad, general statement which describes the operational philosophy of a correctional organization."

From these definitions we can see that, generally speaking, the mission statement broadly addresses the following (Dupree, 1990):

- the organization's constituencies
- the organization's responsibilities to its constituencies and each constituencies responsibilities to the organization
- the role of the organization in the criminal justice system
- the role of the organization in the community

A mission statement is important because it reveals the vision of the organization's managers and employees and is the foundation upon which policies, procedures, and objectives rest. A mission statement identifies what an organization wants to do in the long term and who it wants to serve. The statement should motivate employees; it should establish a general organizational attitude, explain how resources are allocated, and impart the vision of the leaders and elected officials.

DEVELOPING A MISSION STATEMENT

A mission statement captures the organizational philosophy, goals, and visions. Developing a mission statement is often tricky since the general philosophy, goal, and vision of a policy is developed in a political setting. This is exactly why it is so important for practitioners to understand the policy cycle and political process. As we explored extensively in Part II of this text, the politics of crime produce conflicting views as to what causes crime and consequently what to do about crime. In spite of the disagreement over what to do, there is an overwhelming consensus that government needs to have a crime policy. Because of the politics of the crime issue, criminal justice practitioners often are asked to implement policies with conflicting philosophies, goals, and objectives.

Thus, the ability of criminal justice agency personnel to develop clear mission statements is severely limited by conflicting forces outside of the agency's immediate control. Agency personnel must be able to recognize the political aspects of the policy to be implemented and respond appropriately when developing mission statements. If criminal justice agency personnel identify conflicting policy goals and objectives, then officials can at least better understand what prompted government directives.

Agencies may not be able to ignore conflicting orders, but at least they can be in a position to foresee implementation problems and be better equipped to manage personnel who are pulled in two or more directions at the same time. Do not assume that problems in developing mission statements are solely due to outside political forces. Much of the difficulty in developing a mission statement stems from problems that can occur within the agency. Individual employees may see the role of the organization in a different light or at least somewhat differently than their colleagues. Therefore, when writing a mission statement, it is of the utmost importance to gain a measure of consensus among employees in regard to what the organization aims to accomplish.

One important but often overlooked factor is input from the community. Dupree (1990) points out that representatives of government, other criminal justice agencies, community agencies, and the public should be actively encouraged to participate in the success of the organization. This can be accomplished by the creation of a community advisory committee that reflects the makeup of the community. This committee can be an active participant in the development of a mission statement, or its input can be made via the administrator who sits in on both the advisory committee's meetings and the agency's meetings.

Obtaining consensus on a mission statement takes a good deal of time and requires numerous discussions of the issues. Discussions are complicated by the fact that positions taken on issues must be consistent with the law, accrediting agencies such as the International Association of Chiefs of Police or the American Correctional Association, and criminal justice court-related decisions. Inevitably, compromise must occur to meet a complicated list of criteria.

There is no established format, but we can use certain criteria to aid us in our deliberations and writing. Dupree (1990) is helpful in this regard. He asserts that the following criteria must be met:

- *Have a broad focus.* No mission statement should attempt to address all issues. Only key concerns that are broad in scope should be addressed. Writers should never include elements of day-to-day operations.
- *Be concise.* A major difficulty for bureaucrats is to be concise in their writing. However painful it is, the mission statement should be written as simply as possible. If at all possible, it should be limited to one paragraph.
- *Be clear and unmistakable.* Avoid jargon peculiar to the agency. The mission statement should be understandable to people outside of the agency who have no knowledge of law enforcement, courts, or corrections.
- *Impart a vision.* The mission statement should reflect the organization's future and not its past. The statement should convey a shared vision of the future and the overall philosophy of the organization.
- *Be realistic and attainable.* The goals and philosophy stated or implied in the statement must be realistic and attainable.
- *Be positive.* The mission statement defines the future of the organization and therefore must be positive and focus on what will be done and not what cannot be done.

Once the leaders and managers have decided to develop a mission statement, the task can be approached in one of two ways. The first is to adequately train the division or department heads on the specifics of developing a mission statement. They then will work with their subordinates to write the mission statement. The division or department heads will then meet together with the chief executive officer and rewrite the mission statement to incorporate the input of the divisions or departments.

The second way is to convene the department heads or division heads to write a mission statement. The leaders then return to their areas and share the results with subordinates, request feedback, and make suggestions for revision. The managers will then meet together with the chief executive officer and rewrite the statement, incorporating the input of the various departments or divisions.

While neither approach is superior, the first is perhaps the most inclusive. When input is solicited from members of the organization from the beginning, the employees have a chance for original input and opposition is negated by that input. In the second approach, employees may feel that what they say will matter little, and that they are only being asked to co-sign what the managers and leaders have already determined.

In looking at the mission statements of various criminal justice organizations posted on their web sites, we learned that many agencies go to additional lengths to spell out their mission and even articulate certain values that are held most dear. For example, the Georgia Department of Corrections states on their website that the department's vision is as follows: (http://www .dcor.state.ga.us/ABOUTGDC/Mission.html)

> The Georgia Department of Corrections is the best corrections system in the nation at protecting citizens from convicted offenders and at providing effective opportunities for offenders to achieve positive change. We are a leader and partner in making Georgia a safer, healthier, better educated, growing, and best managed state. We accomplish this by:
>
> • Ensuring public safety
> • Operating safe and secure facilities
> • Providing effective community supervision of offenders
> • Creating opportunities for restoration to offenders
> • Ensuring the rights of victims
> • Partnering with public, private, and faith-based organizations
> • Sustaining core values of Loyalty, Duty, Respect, Selfless Service, Honor, Integrity, and Personal Courage
> • Ensuring the well being of employees and their families

The New York City Police Department Patrol Services Bureau has a mission statement that states:

> To protect life and property, reduce crime, improve the quality of life while dealing with the citizens of this city with courtesy, professionalism, and respect.
>
> Direct, coordinate and control the efforts of seven patrol boroughs and the Special Operations Division.
>
> Provide sufficient uniformed patrol officers to respond to emergencies, minimize harm, and maximize public safety.
>
> Deploy resources to effectively combat crime and respond to community needs for police services.
>
> Observe and evaluate performance, equipment and training of field personnel.

The South Dakota Department of Corrections states:

> To protect the citizens of South Dakota by providing safe and secure facilities for juvenile and adult offenders committed to our custody by the courts, to provide opportunities for their rehabilitation, and to provide effective community supervision upon their release.

The New York Department of Corrections formerly had a rather lengthy statement that violated the premise of being concise and was somewhat too narrow in the view of the authors. However, in the past five years they have revised the mission statement which now conforms more to the opinions of the authors. The new mission statement reads thus:

To provide for public protection by administering a network of correctional facilities that:

- Retain inmates in safe custody until released by law;
- Offer inmates an opportunity to improve their employment potential and their ability to function in a non-criminal fashion;
- Offer staff a variety of opportunities for career enrichment and advancement; and,
- Offer stable and humane "community" environments in which all participants, staff and inmates, can perform their required tasks with a sense of satisfaction.

Clearly, an effective mission statement should generate positive feelings and emotions towards an organization. A good mission statement creates the impression that the organization is successful, knows where it is going, is worthy of one's time and support, and is a worthwhile investment on the part of the employee and the taxpayer.

POLICIES AND PROCEDURES

The policies and procedures manual is perhaps the most important document in the organization. The manual serves a number of purposes:

- It produces consistency, efficiency, and professionalism by standardizing the methods by which such responsibilities are accomplished.
- Policies and procedures set clear boundaries for jobs so that each employee knows in advance what response he or she will get from others when making decisions.
- It is an effective mechanism to formally introduce new ideas and concepts to employees.
- It offers a means for the transfer of authority and responsibility for the accomplishment of organizational goals and objectives to staff.
- It is the foundation for staff training.
- It is an important form of documentation for an organizational defense against lawsuits filed by citizens.

- It offers managers a means of control in advance.
- Without clearly written policies and procedures, the organization is unable to receive accreditation from an appropriate agency.

POLICY

Building on what we learned in Chapter 3, we can think of a policy as a standing plan that furnishes broad, general guidelines for channeling management's thinking towards taking action that is consistent with organizational objectives (Certo, 1985). Certo focuses on the attainment of organizational objectives. Pressman and Wildavsky (1973) assert that policies contain both the goal and the means for attainment. Policies also imply theory: "Policies point to a chain of causation between initial conditions and future consequences" (Pressman and Wildavsky, 1973). They point out that policies become programs when we attempt to do something about a particular problem.

Problems are the focus of standards articulated by such organizations as the International Association of Chiefs of Police (IACP) and the American Correctional Association (ACA). A number of lawsuits that questioned policy and procedure have been filed against agencies. For example, in perhaps the best-known case, the Texas Department of Corrections was the defendant in a class-action suit challenging a number of policies and procedures. After a prolonged legal battle, the department agreed to changes such as elimination of the building tender system, but continued the fight through the appeal process and informal resistance to mandated change.

As a result of many such battles, most of which were not as spectacular or expensive, both the International Association of Chiefs of Police and the American Correctional Association have implemented programs that attempt to upgrade the performance of police and correctional organizations by promoting guidelines for the development of polices and procedures.

Organizational policies and procedures are based upon values. Values are qualities that are prized or believed to be good or of benefit to the individual or group (Houston, 1995). In criminal justice, values reflect a system of beliefs and goals shared by fellow workers and the community. For example, solidarity is a value of police officers. Clearly, the value of solidarity is based upon the notion that one needs to trust, and have the trust of fellow officers because of the potential for danger and the need to have capable and trusted colleagues who can be counted upon in the heat of conflict.

The patrol policy of the Multnomah County (Oregon) Sheriff's Department reflects a value of order. In the matter of patrol operations, the need for routine patrols is taken as a given, and who works what patrol beat, who assigns officers a patrol beat, and any exceptions are articulated. The Skokie (Illinois) Police Department policy on patrol shares the vision, of who is served, and services to be rendered to the citizens of Skokie, Illinois. Neither policy is wrong; each one reflects the orientation of the department and presumably, community values. Each in its own way is a broad outline and a general guide to action.

Cultural values also play a role in the articulation of policies and procedures. Our society holds certain values regarding safety, punishment of wrongdoers, and rehabilitation. Those values have undergone a change in recent years, although not as radical a change as some would have us believe. Nevertheless, a policies and procedures manual that reflects the values of the dominant society will be effective whereas one that does not will not be effective.

PROCEDURES

A procedure is a step-by-step outline of activities necessary to fulfill the policy. If the policy is a broad general outline, then the procedure is a specific how-to approach to achieving organizational objectives. Some procedures are short and to the point; others are quite detailed and run to several pages. For example, the procedure for an off-duty police officer to report for duty in times of large-scale disaster such as an airplane crash would read something like the following:

> No officer shall respond to the location of any major emergency or disaster while off duty without reporting to his duty station assignment first. If ordered to report to assist at the scene of an incident, the officer shall respond under the command of an officer in charge of the incident.
>
> If the normal duty station is inoperative, the officer shall contact by phone, if possible, any other section of the department for instruction. A command post will be established for officers to contact by the ranking on-duty officer.

Clearly, in the above example, the officer reading the procedure would have no doubt about what to do if he or she heard a media report of a sudden disaster to which he or she would be obligated to respond. This points to the necessity for clearly written procedures that are unambiguous and succinct. When procedures are clear, everyone wins—the employee, the public, and the inmate or the subject of arrest or questioning.

In comparing the policies and procedures of the two organizations, we recognize a difference—the Multnomah County Sheriff's Department allows more discretion to the individual officer. The Sheriff depends upon the professionalism and knowledge of the craft by the individuals to carry them through the shift. Other departments may leave less individual discretion. The officer is informed of the objectives, functions, specific duties, and even the equipment necessary for proper execution of his or her job. Again, neither is more correct than the other. Each simply reflects the values and orientation of the department's leadership and the community.

RULES

Expertise counts for a great deal in criminal justice agencies. It is the major tool available to control employees and elected officials, and it gives the agencies a measure of power over the public. When writing policies and procedures, it is important to know the difference between policies, procedures, and rules. Policies and procedures are defined above. A rule is defined as "a standing plan that designates specific required action" (Certo, 1985). A rule, for example, might specify that all employees must notify their supervisors at least sixty minutes prior to the beginning of each shift if they are unable to report for work because of illness. Another rule could be, "All officers will report for role call fifteen minutes prior to shift change."

WRITING POLICIES AND PROCEDURES

Involving all staff in the writing of policies and procedures is of the utmost importance. If staff does not have the opportunity to participate, they may feel that the policy and procedures have been imposed from above and passively resist implementation. As a consequence, the time involved in staff involvement is well worth while.

Dupree and Milosovich (1980) offer guidance for criminal justice practitioners and consultants planning to develop policies and procedures. They point out that once policies and procedures are developed and written, staff members who were involved in the process not only understand them but also are aware of alternatives that were considered and rejected, as well as the reasons for rejection. In addition, staff have a sense of responsibility for making the implemented policies and procedures work.

Many criminal justice executives overlook the fact that there is tremendous potential just waiting to be tapped within the organization. The effective manager understands that entrepreneurial spirit and puts it to work for the agency. Dupree and Milosovich (1980) assert that task forces serve as the best method of writing policies and procedures and are also the best method of involving the largest number of people in the process. Using task forces as the primary unit, the following activities most assuredly can be covered for all criminal justice agencies:

- Identifying of policy and procedure topic items
- Collecting and analyzing available resource documents related to specific policy issues
- Developing initial (and if necessary subsequent) drafts of policies and procedures
- Validating the accuracy and sequencing of procedural steps
- Administering the policy
- Involving support services

For corrections agencies, the above activities should be done as well as

- Designing and implementing programs and
- Ensuring security

For law enforcement, the above activities should be completed along with

- Patrolling
- Investigating
- Dealing with juveniles
- Establishing and operating special units

In an endeavor as important as the development and writing of policies and procedures, a person must be appointed as the coordinator for the process. This is important for at least two reasons: it establishes accountability, and someone is designated to assure the timely completion of tasks and select personnel to work on the various task forces. ACA's Planning and Design Guide for Secure Adult and Juvenile Facilities, by Leonard Witke, ed., 2000, published by ACA, Lanham, MD offers a number of suggestions in this arena, as does Martin L. Drapkin's book: *Developing Policies and Procedures for Jails: A Step by Step Guide*, 1996 published by ACA, Lanham, MD.

The size of each task force should be limited to a number that maximizes cooperation and communication; and should not be less than three persons or more than seven (Dupree and Milosovich, 1980). Members of each task force should be selected for their talents rather than their position in the organization. It is also helpful to have individuals from outside the organization serve on the task force if appropriate. For example, in writing policies and procedures for a police department, it may be helpful, especially with a small department, to have a member of the juvenile court participate to streamline the procedures for handling police reports and petitions for juveniles.

Task forces can be made up of employees who are detailed to the task force full time, employees who are detailed to the task force part time, and full-time employees who are asked to serve for a short period of time (either full time or part time) to take advantage of their specific expertise. The important thing to remember is that once the policies and procedures are completed, it is necessary to disband the task force and return the members to their regular duties.

THE CHIEF EXECUTIVE AND POLICIES AND PROCEDURES

The chief executive officer of the organization or agency rarely should be directly involved in the writing of the policies and procedures if he or she wants them to reflect accuracy and to be unbiased in favor of excellence. This is difficult for some chief executive officers because there are certain ways they want the organization to operate. As a consequence, the chief executive officer needs to lead from behind. But, it is the supervisors and line staff that have the expertise, the day-to-day knowledge of how the organization should be managed, and are able to recognize changes that need to be made that will increase efficiency than the employees who actually run the organization?

What is important for the chief executive officer to know is that without his or her support and daily input, the polices and procedures cannot be formulated and articulated. After the manual, or portions of it, has been completed in the first rough draft, the chief executive officer can review the product and suggest changes. Caution should be exercised in approaching suggested changes. Naturally, some changes will reflect the bias and preference of the chief executive officer, but most should not be forced upon the members of the task force. Rather, if the chief executive officer has a question about a certain policy or procedure, he or she should ask why it was drawn up that way if it differs from established procedure. The input of members should be solicited from and if there is no logical reason to argue the point, the chief executive officer should acquiesce to the task force. No procedure, and perhaps few policies, are set in granite. If after a six-month trial period the policy or procedure is found to be unworkable, it can be rewritten.

SUMMARY

The mission statement and the policies and procedures are perhaps the most important documents in an organization. Without them, the members of the organization and the public may have no clear idea what the organization is attempting to do, who it may serve, and where the organization is going. The mission statement should be written clearly and concisely and impart a vision. It should be broad in scope, and the philosophy and goals that are articulated should be realistic and attainable.

Policies and procedures are driven by a mission statement. A policy is a general guide to action. It should provide a roadmap to the future by providing a general outline for action and making decisions consistent with reaching the objectives of the organization. Procedures, on the other hand, are the repetitive steps necessary for achieving specific objectives. Criminal justice practitioners face difficulty, however, if the legislation they are asked to implement is too vague, contains conflicting goals, and is too politically motivated. Yet, practitioners must proceed to the best of their ability and develop organizational policy that attempts to meet stated goals (and sometimes the implied goals) of the legislation.

In writing the mission statement and the policies and procedures, it is necessary for the chief executive officer of the organization to support the task and to take an active hand in the process without dominating it. Therefore, it is important for the chief executive officer to appoint a person to oversee the process and to guide the implementation of the policies and procedures, especially if the chief executive is new to the organization. A task force, or task forces, should be appointed by those with authority to make appointments to formulate and write the policies and procedures. Members can be fulltime, temporary full time, part time, or temporary part time. It is important that all members of the organization have input into the process.

REVIEW QUESTIONS

1. Define the following concepts:
   a. Mission statement
   b. Policy
   c. Procedure
   d. Rule
2. Should a policy be broad brush or narrow in scope? Explain your answer.
3. Why is a policies and procedures manual important to an organization?
4. Identify two accrediting agencies that promote policies and procedures manuals and assist in writing them.
5. Should the chief executive officer take an active role in the writing of policies and procedures? Why?

Chapter Six

Planning and the Policy Process

LEARNING OBJECTIVES

In this chapter, you will do the following:

1. Learn the basics of the planning process
2. Acquire minimal tools for effective policy planning
3. Learn the difference between strategic planning and tactical planning
4. Learn the role of the chief executive in the planning process
5. Understand how planning is necessary for effective policy formulation and implementation

INTRODUCTION

Planning can be defined as the process of arranging future activities to accomplish a particular objective. Certo (1985) defines planning as "the process of determining how the organization can get where it wants to go." Planning functions also include defining goals and the means to achieve them. They also assert that the planning function can be broken into four parts:

1. Establishing goals and fixing their priority
2. Forecasting future events that can affect goal accomplishment
3. Making the plans operational through budgeting
4. Starting and implementing policies that direct the organization's efforts towards the desired ends

Generally speaking, all planning is directed towards improved decision making and is the first step in the decision-making process. Improved planning and the resultant improvement in decision making have several benefits:

- Programs and services are improved. The ultimate goal for any criminal justice organization is service—service to the community and to citizens and inmates or clients.
- The ability to identify and analyze problems is enhanced. Adequate planning generates data and information that can be used to improve decision making.
- Planning demands that clear and attainable objectives be established. Once objectives are established, the procedures to attain them can be specified, as can the linkages between the objectives.
- Cooperation and coordination between the various units or departments is improved.
- Planning allows for effective allocation of resources. In an often resource-scarce environment, it is imperative that the manager establish priorities for the allocation of resources.
- Effective planning precedes policy formation. The planning process lays the groundwork for policies that meet the needs of the organization and the target group. In addition, planning decreases risk within the organization and ensures the safety and well-being not only of officers, staff, and inmates or clients, but also the community. It decreases the risk that requested funds will be cut for the coming year, if cutting them would be detrimental to the organizational mission.
- Planning also decreases the risk involved in accomplishing stated goals.
- Finally, planning decreases the risk that the careers of aspiring, upwardly mobile executives and mid-level managers will be terminated.

There are other reasons for planning. As previously pointed out, planning allows the chief executive to coordinate decision making. In most instances, prisons are custodially oriented institutions, where all decisions are made with a view to security. Likewise, law enforcement agencies subordinate decisions to public safety and the well-being of officers. However, many police managers view planning as "clerical" and not "real police work" (Swanson, Territo, and Taylor, 1993). In recent years, however, more agencies are employing the corporate model of management in corrections and law enforcement. Thus, in the evolution from the charismatic model, or focus on individual traits, to the corporate model, departments in the organization are likely to be managed by competent men and women who are able to make a contribution to the organization but whose functions may be perceived as being in conflict with what many line officers and staff view as the way things ought to be done.

Planning also forces the executive staff to formulate objectives. Pursuing those objectives requires a coordinated effort throughout the organization, with executive staff thinking of how decisions affect the organization. Finally, planning forces the staff to be future-oriented. The advantage of planning is that staff is required to look to the future, anticipate problems or issues, and ponder possible solutions before problems erupt. Mintzberg (1994) points out that planners, and by implication chief executive officers, have been notably reluctant to study their own efforts and that they have been so busy calling on others to gather data that they are uncertain whether they are hitting the mark. Further, he points out, planning can be inflexible and stifle creativity and breed resistance to strategic thinking and novel ideas.

The State of Corrections Planning Today

Burt Nanus (1974) calls our attention to the fact that criminal justice agencies tend to be reactive rather than future-oriented in their decision making and operations. He offers a model that organizes the planning function. If his advice had been taken seriously by criminal justice agencies over the last several years, many of the problems we face today might have been avoided. The planning process is complex, and there are at least five types of planning, as shown in figure 6.1, that should occur in a continuous and systematic fashion.

Few examples of inquiries into the state of the planning functions exist in criminal justice agencies, but one by Houston (1995) illustrates that the planning function was not taken seriously by many corrections departments around the nation. While there were a few scattered examples of excellence in planning, the picture was somewhat gloomy. Figure 6.2 shows the state of planning in most state departments of corrections as well as in New York City, Philadelphia, and Washington, D.C. as it was in 1990.

Forty-three departments of corrections responded to a questionnaire in the spring of 1990. The size of the organizations responding ranged from vary large to very small. In spite of the diversity of responding departments, all chief executive officers who responded either agreed or strongly agreed that planning is important to the future of their agencies. However, at the same time, it appears that departments did not place much emphasis on planning. Some agencies did not have a separate planning department. Most respondents had a planning department as well as a published mission statement and master plan.

Beyond that, the survey revealed a mixed emphasis on planning. For example, in an attempt to determine the depth and breadth of the planning

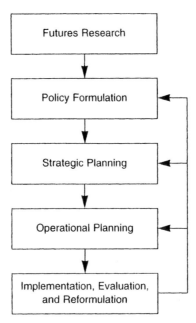

Figure 6.1.   Criminal Justice Planning

process, one question asked, "Do you have long-range plans for increasing numbers of inmates with histories of drug and alcohol abuse, gangs, AIDS, and increasing numbers of elderly inmates?" There were slightly more "no" answers (112) than "yes" (91). It appears that most departments were prepared to meet the demands of drug and alcohol abuse as well as AIDS. Geriatrics and surprisingly gangs were not so well addressed, but with the increasing attention given to gangs since 1990, many agencies now have plans to deal with prison gangs (Knox, et al., 1996). In addition, the size of the overall budget appeared to have little to do with planning or the size of the planning department. Additionally, interface with other agencies that could help in the planning process was nearly nonexistent, as was training for the planners.

Management by Objectives

All organizations want to keep on track and work towards goals. Whether goals are established by work teams, departments, or the organization as a whole, it is important to involve everyone in the process. Once goals or objectives are established, they offer a yardstick against which to measure the organization's progress over time.

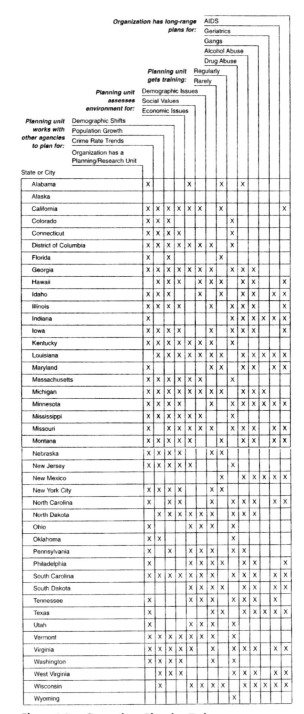

State or City	Organization has a Planning/Research Unit	Crime Rate Trends	Population Growth	Demographic Shifts	Economic Issues	Social Values	Demographic Issues	Rarely	Regularly	Drug Abuse	Alcohol Abuse	Gangs	Geriatrics	AIDS
Alabama	X			X		X		X						
Alaska														
California	X	X	X	X	X	X		X						X
Colorado	X	X	X						X					
Connecticut	X	X	X	X					X					
District of Columbia	X	X	X	X	X	X	X		X					
Florida	X		X						X					
Georgia	X	X	X	X	X	X	X		X	X	X			
Hawaii		X	X	X		X	X	X		X	X			X
Idaho	X	X	X			X			X	X	X		X	
Illinois	X	X	X	X			X		X	X	X			X
Indiana	X								X	X	X	X	X	X
Iowa	X	X	X	X			X		X	X				X
Kentucky	X	X	X	X	X	X	X		X					
Louisiana		X	X	X	X	X	X	X		X	X	X	X	X
Maryland	X						X	X		X	X		X	X
Massachusetts	X	X	X	X	X	X			X					
Michigan	X	X	X	X	X	X	X	X		X	X	X		
Minnesota	X	X	X	X			X		X	X	X	X	X	X
Mississippi	X	X	X	X	X	X			X					
Missouri	X		X	X	X	X	X		X	X	X		X	X
Montana	X	X	X	X	X		X		X	X			X	X
Nebraska	X	X	X	X		X	X							
New Jersey	X	X	X	X	X				X					
New Mexico									X	X	X	X	X	X
New York City	X	X	X	X			X	X						
North Carolina	X		X	X			X		X	X	X		X	X
North Dakota		X	X	X	X	X	X		X	X	X			
Ohio	X				X	X	X		X					
Oklahoma	X	X							X					
Pennsylvania	X		X		X	X	X		X	X				
Philadelphia	X				X	X	X	X		X	X			X
South Carolina	X	X	X	X	X	X	X		X	X	X		X	X
South Dakota					X	X	X	X		X	X		X	X
Tennessee	X				X	X	X		X	X	X		X	
Texas	X						X	X		X	X	X	X	X
Utah	X				X	X	X		X					
Vermont	X	X	X	X	X	X	X		X					
Virginia	X	X	X	X	X		X		X	X	X		X	X
Washington	X	X	X	X			X		X					
West Virginia		X	X	X					X	X	X		X	X
Wisconsin		X			X	X	X	X		X	X	X	X	X
Wyoming									X					

Figure 6.2.   Corrections Planning Today

Management by Objectives (MBO) is generally attributed to Peter Drucker and is "a well-known philosophy of management that assesses an organization and its members by how well they achieve specific goals that superiors and subordinates have jointly established" (Robbins, 1987). Its use is not universal, and police agencies have been slow to adopt management by objectives (Swanson et al., 1993).

Corrections also has been slow to adopt management by objectives, and the above-mentioned study by Houston (1995) included an unreported section on management by objectives. Out of the forty-three agencies that responded, twenty-four did not use management by objectives. The survey asked about the importance of establishing objectives every twelve months; nineteen either agreed or strongly agreed that objectives should be established every twelve months, and fewer still agreed or strongly agreed that biannual or quarterly management by objectives meetings are important. Thus, we can conclude that management by objectives has a long way to go in corrections before it is adopted as an approach to effective management.

There is some discussion in the literature whether management by objectives should be a top-down or a bottom-up approach. In a top-down approach, objectives are formulated by top management and then imposed on line and supervisory staff. In a bottom-up approach, objectives are formulated by supervisors and line staff and given to top management. In Houston's study, of those who answered the question, twenty out of forty-three respondents state that department heads and wardens formulate the objectives.

The consensus in the literature, and by many practitioners, seems to be that a compromise is best. Organizations have multiple goals that compete and sometimes appear to be incompatible. This is especially so in a criminal justice organization where the interests of management, staff, and the public or inmates often conflict, and those conflicts must be resolved and priorities established. One author has concluded that organizational objectives should be treated "as fiction produced by an organization to account for, explain, or rationalize its existence to particular audiences rather than as valid and reliable indications of purpose" (Warriner, 1965). Thus, it is important to involve as many staff as possible and to develop a living document that reflects the real organization and not an organization the managers think a particular audience wants to see.

ESTABLISHING OBJECTIVES

Chapter 5 stressed the importance of the mission statement—it provides a direction for the organization. From the mission statement, one may derive goals and objectives. Often, the words *goals* and *objectives* are used interchangeably, but experts usually agree that a goal is more general than is an objective (More and O'Neill, 1984). For example, a police agency may establish a goal of reducing burglaries in a particular neighborhood. An objective would be to establish a Neighborhood Watch Program in that neighborhood and enroll 40 percent of the households in the program.

The management by objectives process is a lengthy one that may require years to put finally in place. Goals and objectives need to be reviewed periodically so that progress or attainment of objectives can be judged. In addition, everyone in the organization should feel some ownership of the program.

According to Certo (1985) managers can increase the quality of their objectives by following certain guidelines:

1. Managers should allow the people responsible for attaining the objectives to have a voice in setting them. Line staff often have a better feel for conditions than top management; therefore, their input is crucial if work-related problems faced by line staff are going to be translated into meaningful objectives.
2. Managers should state objectives as specifically as possible, as precise language minimizes confusion. Further, objectives should be unambiguous, prioritized, measurable, and most of all, attainable.
3. Managers should relate objectives to specific actions, whenever necessary. Specific actions eliminate the need for guesswork on the part of those responsible for achieving objectives.
4. Managers will know when they have achieved results. Completion of a cell house renovation before a deadline is cause for celebration. Likewise, a decrease in crime in a specific neighborhood can be a source of pride.
5. Managers should set goals high enough so that employees will have to strive to meet them, but not so high that employees become discouraged and give up trying.
6. Managers should specify when they expect goals to be achieved. Stated timeframes are important so that employees can pace themselves.
7. Managers should set objectives only in relation to other organizational objectives. Keeping a close eye on the larger picture will keep conflicting objectives to a minimum.
8. Managers should state objectives clearly and simply. Understandable and concise language should be used when communicating a goal to the organization.

While there may be problems in formulating and implementing a management-by-objectives program, Kast and Rosenzweig (1979) point out:

[M]anagement by objectives programs have been used successfully by a number of business organizations to integrate organizational and individual goals. The most successful programs appear to be those that emphasize a total systems approach to management by objective and take into consideration its impact on all of the organization's subsystems.

Hazards in Planning

Often, planning is doomed to failure even if the chief executive supports planning activities. Paul J. Stonich (1975) calls our attention to three reasons why planning efforts fail:

1. A focused approach to planning is often lacking. Organizations often concentrate on specific actions and decisions but fail to develop a planning system that brings important issues to the attention of the planners.
2. Many formal planning systems do not concentrate on actions or decisions that managers can take today to influence performance tomorrow. Instead, Stonich points out, technicians take over and emphasize overly analytical techniques, statistics, and other analytical tools that have no meaning for the action-oriented manager.
3. Many organizations are guilty of separating formal planning from the rest of the management systems, which include organizing, communicating, reporting, evaluating, and conducting a performance review. If planning is to be effective, it must be an integral part of the total organization.

More and O'Neil (1984) also point out a number of "landmines" of which the planner must be aware:

- *Gathering excessive data.* Planners often become obsessed with data. One should determine in advance the data necessary to make a decision.
- *Misinterpretation of data.* Do not be afraid to seek expert help in interpreting data.
- *Inadequate definition of the problem.* If boundaries are not defined, the problem takes on a life of its own and the planner becomes lost in a forest of trivia.
- *Lack of understanding of the criminal justice system.* The planner must have a good working knowledge of the criminal justice system to be an effective planner.
- *Establishment of irrelevant objectives.* All objectives should be quantified and bound by time restraints.
- *Premature acceptance of a plan without considering the alternatives.* There is more than one solution to problems and the planner should be aware of those alternatives or at least know how to get at them.

- *Improper allocation to solution resources.* Due to the misallocation of resources in any agency, work on the most critical problems or objectives first.
- *Lack of criteria for appraisal.* Objectives should be based on some performance criteria.
- *Insufficient emphasis on planning organization.* The planner should be aware of the planning function and not take on extraneous duties that will take time and resources away from the planning function.
- *Lack of coordination with other activities.* Ascertaining relationships with other agencies will aid in the planning and implementation process.

Overall, planning offers distinct advantages if it is used properly and if executives are able to delegate and not devote an inordinate amount of time to it themselves. If processes are kept simple and planning flows from a coherent management by objectives program, then the obvious conclusion is that the advantages of planning certainly outweigh its disadvantages.

Managing the Planning System

The planning process contains seven steps. It is difficult to put them in any kind of order because they are interrelated:

1. Identify the planning manager/coordinator. While the chief executive must focus on long-range strategic planning, he or she cannot, in most cases, spend the bulk of his or her time on planning and implementing the plans. Therefore, it is important to identify one person who will be responsible for managing the planning unit and acting as the liaison with the various departments during all stages of the process, particularly during the implementation process.
2. Identify and state institutional organization objectives. It is necessary to clearly spell out the objectives of the organization before the planning process begins.
3. List ways to achieve the objectives. In a criminal justice environment, there is often more than one alternative.
4. Choose the best way to achieve the objective. Choosing the best way includes examining the needs of the public, officers, and support personnel. In addition, it is a good idea to review court decisions or pending legislation.
5. Identify the department or division heads who will be responsible for reaching the objective. Accountability is vital, so it is important for department heads to know what they are supposed to do and when they are supposed to do it.

6. Develop plans to pursue the chosen alternative. Once an alternative is chosen, the responsible department head must develop strategic and tactical plans.
7. Put the plans into action. Obviously, there is no benefit to the organization until the plans are put into action. All plans need to include strategic and tactical strategies that include the entire organization.

Tools for Planning

Crime is a pressing social problem and it is up to competent managers in law enforcement, courts, and corrections to devise policies and programs that meet the need for public safety. In addition, criminal justice managers must be well informed when called upon by legislators and others in the public sector who are interested in public safety and need advice and information. An effective planning unit in the organization will aid in this process and allow the criminal justice manager to offer suggestions for programs and policy formation based upon facts not opinion or feelings.

For example, the chief of police or commissioner of corrections should begin each planning year by establishing the relationship between crime, demographics, economic conditions, and social indicators. Second, he or she and relevant staff should attempt to determine the impact of new legislation, social trends, and demographics on the crime rate and/or the prison population.

Third, they should estimate the potential for developing new programs and new institutions or facilities. Finally, they should evaluate existing programs to determine whether they should be continued. To accomplish these ends, effective planners need to be armed with tools that further their ability to do the job well (Gibbons, et al., 1977).

Core Knowledge

Criminal justice planners should be knowledgeable about contemporary philosophy in law enforcement and/or corrections' procedures, as well as trends in programs. This means that they should have a minimum of a bachelor's degree in criminal justice or a related field.

Sources of Criminal Justice Data and Other Information

- Hudzik and Cordner (1983) note that "an essential element in planning is data—data about past and present conditions, about goals, forecasts, and alternatives for the future." However, crime statistics are notoriously unreliable for several reasons: reporting varies from one jurisdiction to another;

reporting is often voluntary for each agency; and often changes over time in reporting procedures further distort the statistics. Nevertheless, information sources are available to aid the planner, including:

- U.S. Census
- U.S. Census of Manufacturers
- National Crime Survey
- Uniform Crime Reports (UCR)
- Vital Statistics of the United States National Institute of Justice
- Bureau of Justice Statistics' *Sourcebook of Criminal Justice Statistics*
- Various state and local reports

Tools for Scheduling Activities and Use of Resources

Scheduling is the process of compiling lists of tasks and the people and resources necessary to complete them. Two well-known scheduling techniques are Gantt charts and the Program Evaluation and Review Technique (PERT).

GANTT CHART

The Gantt chart, developed by Henry L. Gantt, is essentially a bar graph that shows the time allotment on the horizontal axis and the scheduled resource on the vertical axis. The chart in figure 6.3 depicts the timeframes for Jim, Bill, and Melinda who are assigned tasks relating to opening a new correctional institution. Jim is on schedule in completing his tasks; Bill is one day behind on his task. Melinda, however, has completed her task ahead of schedule and has begun to work on a related task.

A Gantt chart serves several purposes. First, the chart can be used to gain an overview of what tasks are to be completed, when they are to be completed, who is to work on them, and what, if any, resources are to be used. Second, correctional managers may use the Gantt chart to help coordinate organizational resources. Finally, the chart can be used to establish worker output. If workers are completing tasks more quickly than expected, for example, adjustments can be made in the work environment and expectations of productivity

Program Evaluation and Review Technique

PERT is a group analysis and charting procedure that begins by determining the sequences of dependent activities. In 1958, the management firm of Booz, Allen, and Hamilton developed PERT to plan the procedures and processes

Week 10

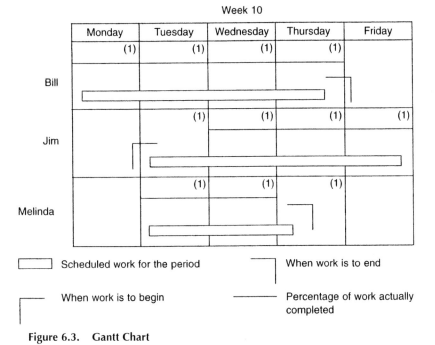

Figure 6.3.   Gantt Chart

required to complete the Polaris Missile Project. The U.S. Air Force, and then the civilian sector, adopted PERT, often under different names, to help them complete complicated projects.

There are four advantages to PERT:

1. It streamlines production.
2. It helps assure that projects will be completed within budget.
3. It promises optimum use at all times of personnel and material resources.
4. It accepts uncertainty as part of the system.

The PERT network contains two elements: activities and events. Activities are specified behaviors and events are completions of major tasks. Certain activities are assigned for each event, and these activities must be completed before that event can materialize. PERT charts are always illustrated from left to right to show how the events are interrelated. In addition, the timeframe is presented on the solid lines, in parentheses.

On a PERT chart, the critical path is the sequence of events and activities that takes the longest time. If problems arise, critical path analysis highlights those areas where remedial action is needed to maintain the overall program

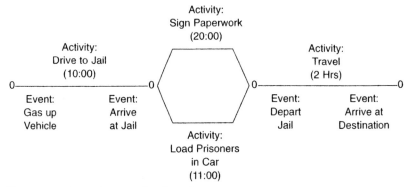

Figure 6.4.   PERT-Transporting the Prisoner

schedule. Figure 6.4 depicts the critical path to completing a simple activity and shows the difference between events and activities. It does not take much imagination to realize how complicated PERT charts could be for opening a new institution. In that instance, there would be many, perhaps several thousand, activities noted, thus helping the planners keep on track.

There are four primary steps in designing a PERT network:

1. List all activities and events for the project and the sequence in which these activities and events need to be completed.
2. Determine how much time will be needed to complete each activity and event.
3. Design the PERT network using the information in steps 1 and 2.
4. Identify the critical path.

Who Plans?

The answer to the question of who plans is very simple—anyone who wants to succeed. This is not to suggest that criminal justice executives do not want to successfully pursue the mission of the organization or to have a successful career; quite the contrary. However, in criminal justice, there are some built-in impediments to planning that do not exist in the private sector as Nanus (1974) points out:

> The main problem seems to be that individual criminal justice agencies tend to be reactive rather than future-oriented in their decision making operations. Systematic and comprehensive long-range planning is seldom done because these agencies are constantly being subjected to short-term political pressures; their funding is based on a one-year cycle; and the problems of the moment are often

real enough and quite compelling. However, even a totally reactive agency can operate even more effectively with a long-range planning perspective, as military strategic planning has often demonstrated. More important, there can be no meaningful regional or systemwide planning without individual agencies first being able to establish their own orderly, systematic, and continuous processes of setting objectives, anticipating the future, and bringing these anticipations to bear on critical present decisions.

Systemwide and Local Planning

On a practical basis, planning can be broken into systemwide and local planning. Systemwide planning refers to planning carried out by what is generally referred to as the central office in corrections, or in the case of law enforcement, either the headquarters office in the state capital or by the main police precinct. Basically, the procedure for planning sessions at the central office level is the same as at the local level.

Usually, the central office for corrections is in the state capital, and the commissioner of corrections is responsible for initiating planning activities. Likewise, the superintendent of state police or the chief of police are concerned with the same issues at the local level, but on a more cosmic scale. They are also concerned with issues such as system crowding, new facilities and equipment, pending or needed legislation, and kindred items. Planning activities must include not only support personnel in the central office but also all subordinate executives.

Local planning is usually initiated by the chief executive officer of the correctional institution or field unit. The chief executive officer usually wants to plan for such issues as increases in crime rates and numbers, changes in traffic patterns, calls for service, and in the case of corrections, inmate-client programs, services such as medical care or food services, and issues relating to inmate management, such as disciplinary reports. While these issues are similar to, and in many ways overlap, the responsibilities of the central office or main precinct, the difference is in their impact on the day-to-day operation of the organization. The development of local plans, by necessity, should include a variety of personnel who have knowledge of the organization and its processes. To begin, a chief of police or warden requests that all department heads meet with their personnel to develop a list of objectives for the coming year, or perhaps for a longer period of time.

Once these objectives and the means to achieve them have been identified, the department heads submit them to the chief or warden, or his or her designee, to be compiled in a master list. Next, the chief executive officer will call all department heads for a joint planning session. Ideally, this session should be held at a location away from the police station or institution so that participants can focus their attention on the matters at hand without interruption. Once an organizational plan is formulated, the plan can be sent to the central office or main precinct for review and for inclusion in systemwide planning.

The Chief Executive and Planning

It is crucial that the warden, chief of police, and all executives support and participate in the planning process. The chief executive has five specific planning responsibilities (Nanus 1997):

1. To assure that a planning mechanism for the agency is developed and maintained.
2. To assure that lower-level executives bring long-range considerations to bear on operational problems.
3. To initiate, stimulate, and evaluate strategic and operational planning.
4. To lead the policy planning effort, particularly regarding setting objectives.
5. To create an environment in which innovation and change are encouraged and rewarded.

For the planning process to be effective, the chief executive of a criminal justice organization must recognize that he or she has many roles. The chief executive is the recognized ceremonial head and must represent the agency at various functions. He or she must assure that organization members are properly guided towards the accomplishment of organizational goals. This person also acts as a liaison with the forces and interests outside the organization, monitors progress towards goals, and settles disputes within the organization. Finally, as a leader and manager, the chief executive officer must assure the proper allocation of scarce resources to accomplish the organization's mission and achieve stated objectives.

Tactical Planning

Tactical planning is short-range, and it focuses on the local organization. Certo (1985) asserts that short-range planning emphasizes current operations of various parts of the organization. Usually, tactical planning will extend only one year or so into the future and will emphasize important but attainable objectives. Tactical plans in law enforcement are often related to patrol, investigation, and crime prevention activities. In corrections, tactical planning usually relates to inmate management, programs, and the physical plant.

For example, the warden and the planning committee of a correctional institution may establish a goal to renovate a cell house within twelve months; another goal might relate to the excessive number of disciplinary reports for the defacing of government property. The warden and planning committee will then develop and define measures and objectives to correct the problem within a certain amount of time. A chief of police may determine that gangs are on the increase in the city and establish a goal to decrease gang membership. He or she then could establish an objective of offering a gang-awareness seminar to all parent-teacher organizations in the city as well as to twenty-five civic groups in the coming year.

Strategic Planning

Strategic planning is the "keystone to effective planning at both the agency and system levels. Without strategic planning, the agency is apt to be directionless and uncoordinated (Hudzik and Cordner, 1983)." Strategic planning is long-range in scope and focuses on the larger organization; in other words, it is usually systemwide. In this case, we can define long range as three to five years or even longer, in spite of the yearly budget cycle. Strategic planning can be defined as the formation, implementation, and evaluation of actions that will enable an organization to achieve its long-range objectives (David, 1986).

According to Gibbons et al. (1977), strategic planning calls for a wealth of knowledge and information in two general categories. First, the planner must possess an in-depth understanding of crime patterns, social forces in crime causation, and key factors in the development of criminal justice philosophy and practices. Second, the planner must possess a command of planning principles, concepts, and tools that can be used to deal with specific problems.

Since criminal justice agencies are an integral part of the community, the manager must develop strategies that aid him or her in developing plans that meet the needs of the community. Certo (1985) proposes environmental analysis to pinpoint environmental factors that influence organizational operations. According to Certo, economic issues, demographics, social values, and suppliers are critical issues to consider when developing strategic plans.

Economic Issues

Economics is the science of how people produce, distribute, and use various goods and services. Economic issues affect not only our everyday lives but also public agencies. Without a steady tax base, for example, funding is apt to be decreased, and this results in eliminating or cutting of programs. Therefore, if a recession or a downturn in the economy is on the horizon, strategic plans should be developed accordingly.

Demographics

Demographics are the characteristics of a population. Changes in the demographics of a state, city, or region can influence a criminal justice organization drastically. For example, the population of youths between twelve and fifteen years of age is going to increase over the next few years. What effect, if any, will this phenomenon have on the delinquency rate, violence, gangs, need for prisons, camps, and related agencies and programs?

Social Values

Social values are relative degrees of worth that society attaches to abstractions such as patriotism, "right," and "wrong." Social values change over time and affect the operations of criminal justice agencies. In recent years, for example, there has been a call for zero tolerance of crime and for harsher sentences and more stringent parole guidelines. This has placed an almost intolerable strain on criminal justice agencies to deliver services.

Suppliers

The criminal justice agency does not function in a vacuum. Suppliers are those businesses and other community agencies that provide the organization with goods, services, inmates, and utilities. Examples of suppliers include the courts, utilities, business equipment suppliers, and food venders. Successful long-term planning must generally include some consideration of price and availability of supplies, and the numbers of crimes and the flow of inmates/clients to the organization.

SUMMARY

Planning is crucial if the organization is to achieve a measure of success. The chief executive officer is responsible for the development and continuation of an executive planning program. Because chief executive officers cannot spend all their time working on planning activities, they must appoint someone as the organization planner. To accomplish the goals set, the planner needs to have certain qualifications, including an ability to easily relate to action-oriented managers. If planning is to be effective, the chief executive officer must develop a mission statement with subordinates to clarify the mission and objectives to be achieved over a specified period of time. Objectives are best arrived at in a team effort that is both top down and bottom up.

Those doing the planning must give attention to both strategic planning and tactical planning. Both are important to the success of the organization. Strategic planning looks to the long term and tactical planning looks at the day-to-day operations of the organization. Planners also should pay attention to economic issues, demographics, social values, and suppliers.

REVIEW QUESTIONS

1. Define planning.
2. Are there benefits to planning? If so, what are they?
3. Do all criminal justice agencies have an effective planning unit?
4. What is management by objectives? Is it really necessary to the planning process?
5. Why can't the chief executive officer handle all the necessary planning for an agency?
6. Describe the difference between strategic and tactical planning.
7. Join with two or three others and develop a PERT chart illustrating how you plan to get home after work or class.

Chapter Seven

Tools for the Criminal Justice Policy Analyst

LEARNING OBJECTIVES

In this chapter, you will:

1. Learn what tools are available to the policy analyst and how to use them.
2. Become familiar with the three tools of input and the matrices available for use.
3. Learn the value of the Quantitative Strategic Planning Matrix.
4. Learn the pitfalls of the policy process.

INTRODUCTION

In chapter 3 we discussed policy inputs as a part of policy formation. It is important that criminal justice practitioners and scholars have input in order to aid in the formation of sensible and effective crime legislation. If we fail to contribute we will continue to see the same tired ideas repackaged again and again for the sake of symbolism rather than for effective action. This chapter gets at the specifics of input and allows the practitioner and/or analyst to make an important contribution.

Planning is a concept to which all criminal justice executives and legislators give lip service, but that often is ignored, much to the detriment of the taxpaying public and the successful implementation of legislation or policy. In chapter 6, we discussed planning and its impact on developing effective policy. In chapter 4 we pointed out that by applying the policy cycle to proposed legislation and policy, the criminal justice CEO will be a player in the policy process rather than being victimized by it. In our view, policy without effective planning does not serve the public interest. Ideally, the criminal justice policy analyst and planner would like to have all necessary tools, knowledge, and techniques to effectively carry out the policy process. This is not usually the case, from Congress and the State House to the station house and the prison; with few exceptions, the policy analyst must operate on a kitchen chair philosophy, that is, with the bare essentials. Nevertheless, the policy analyst can improve the process if he or she is armed with core knowledge of criminal justice and the planning process. Gibbons et al. (1977) point out that the criminal justice planner should be equipped with a wealth of information in three areas. First, the planner should have an in-depth understanding of crime patterns, social forces in crime causation, key factors in the development of criminal careers, and related matters. Their argument is that the government can do very little about crime in the absence of knowledge of the problem about to be attacked. The planner should be aware of any number of societal trends that impact on crime, and those trends should be identified, anticipated, and incorporated into plans and policy.

Second, the policy analyst should have an in-depth knowledge and understanding of the machinery of criminal justice. This includes police operations, court operations, the correctional process, and how programs may influence the recidivism rate. Abstract and metaphorical understandings of the workings of criminal justice will not suffice. The analyst must understand the linkages of the justice operation with various "publics" and interest groups. Additionally, the analyst needs extensive information that identifies the ways in which specific legislators, citizen groups, and other people influence the system. The third category of knowledge required by the policy analyst is a body of planning principles, concepts, and tools that can be utilized to effectively confront specific criminal justice planning and policy problems. This chapter focuses upon the planning process and much more as a prelude to policy formation.

MANAGING AND OBTAINING INFORMATION

In 1987 William Archambeault noted that criminal justice agencies were struggling with the task of coping with the emerging technology of computers and the use of information. The problem, he asserted, was that we were attempting to graft twenty-first-century information technology onto nineteenth-century organizations. In the past twenty years we have traveled far. In fact, the field of informational technology is growing at an incredible pace.

Today's criminal justice practitioner is able to handle a vast amount of information without giving it much thought. Still, without proper information, the public good is not well served and the practitioner is at a disadvantage. For example, the police officer on routine patrol should be able to determine if a traffic violator is wanted in another jurisdiction, the jail administrator must know when the inmate is due for release or if he or she is to be held for another jurisdiction. The probation officer must be able to glean information from a variety of sources in order to write an adequate presentence report. The prison case manager must have information on the inmate if he or she is to make proper decisions relative to security, community programs, and perhaps even release. Thus, information plays a major role in the life of the criminal justice practitioner as well as the policy analyst.

Hudzik and Cordner (1983) point out that the increasing use of information systems in criminal justice reflects the decision-making approach to the improvement of productivity. The effective criminal justice planner and policy analyst must be able to find, manipulate, and store a great deal of information on a daily basis if the organization is to function smoothly and the policy process is to be properly informed. For example, in the late 1990s North Carolina embarked upon an aggressive building program in order to keep up with the increasing numbers of inmates remaining in the system due to changes brought about by structured sentencing as well as increasing numbers of court commitments.

In order to plan and implement policy mandated by legislation, the North Carolina Division of Prisons had to maintain adequate information on numbers of inmates, security needs, risk factors, needs of inmates, and so on if the construction program was to meet the needs of both inmates and the taxpayer. The effective use of information and tools aided the Division of Prisons in its effort to serve the taxpayer. In truth, after careful consideration, if such analysis of information were conducted, it may prove that pursuit of alternatives to prison would serve the taxpayer better. However, since the public and legislators were more motivated by feelings rather than fact, a change in policy is still unlikely. Such careful study of the facts and probable consequences should have been undertaken by the Legislative Research Office, Division of Prisons, and the staff of the individual elected officials who sponsored legislation that was thought to have the potential to drive up the prison population. In order to effectively conduct a search for the facts, there are a number of tools available to aid all corrections policy analysts and executives.

COMPUTERS

Computers have taken over the management of criminal justice agencies. No longer is the question one of, "When are we getting computers?" rather it is now "How soon do we get our upgrade?" The speed with which computers are able to process information as well as the associated benefit of lower cost to maintain information has revolutionized criminal justice organizations. Simple but mundane and repetitive tasks such as keeping personnel records and inventories as well as the more complex tasks of inmate records, assisting in investigations by the police, crime trends and statistics, charting demographic information, identifying latent fingerprints, and compiling mug shots are all made much more simple and easy to manage through the use of computers.

Computers have become almost second nature to most of us by now, and it is difficult to remember how we got along without them. It is difficult to remember that it has only been relatively recently that computers were introduced on a large scale to many criminal justice agencies. It is unthinkable that there are any small police and sheriffs departments that do not use computers, let alone corrections agencies. Managing a police agency, jail, probation department, or prison today is nearly unthinkable without the aid of computers.

A properly constructed management information system (MIS) is necessary for the retrieval of information in order to plan. The MIS is used to store and sort the usual information pertaining to personnel, budgets, law enforcement related information, and inmate classification information. The MIS is also invaluable for storing information relative to the demographics of an inmate population, the population at large, the numbers and types of crimes committed, the location of perpetrators, and where crimes are committed. This is the information necessary for the coherent formulation of criminal justice policy on both the macro and micro level.

A MIS is defined as "a network established within an organization to provide mangers with information that will assist them in decision making" (Certo 1985). The Management Information-System Committee of the Financial Executives Institute provides a more detailed definition of MIS:

> MIS is a system designed to provide selected decision-oriented information needed by management to plan, control, and evaluate the activities of the [organization] corporation. It is designed within a framework that emphasizes profit planning, performance planning, and control at all levels. It contemplates the ultimate integration of required business information subsystems, both financial and nonfinancial, within the company [organization] (Holms 1970).

The MIS is irreplaceable as a tool to aid the policy analyst. There are a number of sources to look up regarding establishing an MIS (see McEwen 1990; Search Group, 1990; Houston 1995; O'Brian and Marakis, 2005), and they are a rich source of information for the policy analyst.

Computer simulation is another tool for the planner. Simulation is usually used when there are a large number of variables, making exploration of each variable impracticable. The planner or policy analyst must have a good grasp of the factors involved and how they interact.

> The process of constructing a simulation reveals the interrelationships among variables, some of which are presumably under the analyst's control. The effect of changing some of these variables can be predicted by changing the computer program accordingly. Assuming that the model is an accurate representation of the way in which factors produce outcomes, the policy consequences of various administrative actions can be predicted with the simulation. The technique is thus particularly valuable when actual experiments on target populations are impractical, unethical, or too slow to be of practical benefit (Hirschhorn 1982).

One such technique is described by Hudzik and Cordner (1983), which was developed for the purpose of explaining the relationships between crime and components of the public sector. Two other models are JUSSIM and JUSSIM II, both of which are case-flow models of the criminal justice system that take into account various types of crimes, their volume, the routes followed by those cases through the system, and the resource requirements created by the case flows. JUSSIM II also takes into account recidivism and allows the planner to use the model interactively (Hudzik and Cordner 1983). The Borland C++ Builder 2006 may have potential for corrections planners and policy formulation. However, it is a very sophisticated program and those without strong computer skills may be hesitant to use it. There are other appropriate scenario programs that can be used.

DATA FOR CRIMINAL JUSTICE PLANNING AND POLICY FORMATION

Mention data to many people and they blanch and immediately conjure up a mental image of complex equations and reams of figures that border on the incomprehensible. While there are people who revel in such precision and readily understand such matters, most criminal justice planners are not quite so sophisticated. However, one such individual should be on the planning staff. Yet, the types of data necessary for effective planning are readily available and quite understandable to the average person.

Data in criminal justice are either qualitative or quantitative. Qualitative data provide information such as race, sex, religious affiliation, and economic status. Such information does not have mathematical qualities. Quantitative data, on the other hand, do have mathematical qualities and are expressed as such. A quick glance through the *Uniform Crime Report* or the *Sourcebook of Criminal Justice Statistics* reveals the type of data available to the criminal justice planner.

Both types of data can be divided into nominal data, ordinal data, interval data, and ratio data. Nominal data have the properties of mutual exclusivity and exhaustiveness; that is, every piece of data collected on a variable fits into one category only. For example, sex is exclusive. One cannot be both male and female. Ordinal data can be mathematically ordered, such as by age, most numerous crimes to the least numerous crimes, and so on. Much research in criminal justice collects ordinal data by use of a Likert Scale asking the respondent to strongly agree, agree, neutral, disagree, or strongly disagree. Such ordinal data are valuable, but do not address the strength of the reply and amount of difference between, for example, strongly agree and agree. Interval data measure the actual distance between categories. Budget figures are often interval data, and crime statistics as measured by age are often expressed as interval data. Finally, ratio data originate from a zero point. Age or budget data have zero points as well.

In planning, there are several types of data. Hudzik and Cordner (1983) suggest the following:

ENVIRONMENTAL DATA

- *Agency missions and goals.* These data are usually qualitative and come from several sources both from within the agency and without
- *Crime.* These data are usually quantitative.
- *Economic and budget condition.* These data are usually expressed quantitatively and often as trends.
- *Population characteristics.* Usually expressed quantitatively along the dimensions of socioeconomics, income, race, housing, education, employment, and so on.
- *Public and political values.* Data are often qualitative and are subjectively derived, and often affect agency goals, its mission, and program options.
- *Labor-market conditions.* This is information on the labor pool from which employees are drawn, as well as law violators and clients/inmates.

ORGANIZATIONAL DATA

- *Work loads.* These data reflect the amount and kind of work performed by the agency, such as man hours consumed on tasks.
- *Job-focused data.* These data and information concern the nature of the work done in an agency and can be defined and divided into jobs that are collections of roles, tasks, and activities.

- *Employee-focused data.* These data focus upon the characteristics of employees, usually describing the numbers of people, age, training and so on.
- *Performance.* These data are usually concerned with how the agency is meeting its obligations, such as arrest rates, clearance rates, numbers of disciplinary reports in prison, segregation population, numbers of probationers violated for technical reasons, and so on.

SYSTEM DATA

- *Simulations of rate and flow.* These are data relating to the intake and flow of offenders into and through the stages of the system.
- *System-transaction data.* These data relate to tracking offenses and offenders through the system itself.

STATISTICS

This text doesn't provide a detailed description of statistics and their applications, but at a basic level there are two types of statistics: *descriptive statistics* and *inductive statistics.* The former refer to statistics that have boiled down a large amount of information to figures that are easy to grasp. Percentages, means, standard deviations, and correlation coefficients reduce the data to manageable proportions. A certain amount of information is lost, and the analyst must be cautious in interpreting the data, but the advantage is that nearly everyone can understand the results.

Inductive statistics, on the other hand, refer to inferences about a larger population that are drawn from information collected from a sample population. Blalock (1979) notes two reasons why this is practical; the most obvious is what he calls the time-cost factor. It is impractical for the researcher, or in our case the planner, to ask every prisoner booked into the county jail if he or she had used drugs in the past seven days. But the researcher can ask a representative sample and make inferences about all prisoners booked into jail. Certain caveats apply, of course, but the researcher can plan for programs based upon the information obtained. Another reason for generalizing from a limited population is because the population is not easily defined. In replicating some research projects in criminal justice, we often hope the generalizations will apply elsewhere under similar circumstances. For example, we may have used all north central states as the unit of analysis for studying gang migration. We may then want to generalize about gang migration in general under similar circumstances.

SOURCES OF INFORMATION

Two types of information are needed for effective planning in the policy process: (1) internal information, which refers to information that is generated from within the organization that informs on the processes at work and about employees, inmates/probationers/parolees, and so on; and (2) external information that informs about the external environment, such as politics, the economy, and general population demographics. Both types of information are necessary for policy formulators and elected officials.

AUDITING THE INTERNAL ENVIRONMENT

In looking to the internal environment, the analyst is interested in what the organization is doing and how the organization is doing its job. There are a number of places to look for information on how the organization is doing its job. For example, court dockets are a rich source of information on who is coming before the court and for what reasons. In addition, a certain amount of information is available about the demographics of defendants who appear before the court.

In probation agencies, client files and agency statistics keep track of violations, program completions, and successful discharge from probation. Prisons are an even richer vein of information. In this day and age, corrections agencies are nearly fanatical about accurate record-keeping. The inmate file contains an abundance of information about the inmate and his or her background. Institutional records will also contain information on inmates committed and those discharged, disciplinary reports, program participation, levels of security, prior records vis-à-vis adjustment in prison, and so on.

Law enforcement agencies are as fanatical about accurate record-keeping as corrections agencies. One can obtain information on numbers of arrests, known crimes by patrol sector, information on victims, as well as personnel information.

AUDITING THE EXTERNAL ENVIRONMENT

The criminal justice organization does not exist in a vacuum; it is a porous organization with often ill-defined boundaries and it is constantly being influenced by events and individuals outside of the organization. For example, changes in legislation can and do impact on the numbers of people prosecuted by the prosecuting attorneys office, thereby causing an increase in the inmate population of the state prison system. Therefore, the policy analyst must anticipate the consequences, both intended and unintended, of proposed policy proposals.

In looking to the external environment for information to inform policy formation, a number of issues are important:

Economic forces
The tax burden on the general population
Government spending deficits
Unemployment trends
Inflation rates
Interest rates
Economies of scale
Price fluctuations in the private sector
Demographic changes in the general population
Things that shape the way citizens think, live, play, and work Political, environmental, and legal forces
Special interest groups ascending or descending in power Rise and fall of political regimes
Court decisions
Technological forces

The above issues are important, but where to look is sometimes a mystery to the planner or policy analyst. Sources include:

ECONOMIC INFORMATION

Economic Outlook
U.S. Bureau of Labor Statistics
Monthly Labor Review
Handbook of Labor Statistics
U.S. Department of Commerce
Business statistics
Long-term economic growth
Kiplinger Washington Letter
Federal Reserve Bulletin
U.S. Bureau of the Census, *Statistical Abstract of the United States* The local Chamber of Commerce

SOCIAL, CULTURAL, AND DEMOGRAPHIC INFORMATION

Uniform Crime Report
Bureau of Justice Statistics
American Statistics Index
All publications of the U.S. Bureau of Census *Demographic Yearbook*
Ford Foundation Report
County Business Patterns
County and city data books
The local Chamber of Commerce
City directories

POLITICAL AND GOVERNMENTAL INFORMATION

Monthly Catalogue of U.S. Governmental Publications *Federal Register*
Congressional Research Office
The various legislative research offices
The local Chamber of Commerce
Professional society publications, such as: *International Association of Chiefs of Police*
State Sheriff's Journal
American Correctional Association

TOOLS FOR THE POLICY ANALYST

A number of tools are available for the policy analyst and planner. Perhaps of most importance are tools for the scheduling of activities such as Gantt Charts and Performance Evaluation and Review Technique (PERT), as discussed in chapter 6.

The tools discussed in this chapter are valuable aids to policy formation and implementation. The policy analyst is in a peculiar position-he or she must be able to keep one eye on the past to see what has gone before and one eye on the future in order to look ahead to implementation. If the policy analyst or agency head is able to accomplish that feat, then he or she will be well on the way to successfully designing policy that serves the taxpayer and the agency. We now turn to a framework that can aid the policy analyst or agency head to formulate sound policy.

MAKING THE SUBJECTIVE OBJECTIVE

Effective policy formation is difficult due to the subjective nature of the task. The analyst is asked to evaluate human, economic, social, and demographic variables and translate them into specifics in order to meet the needs of the constituency. Since we are unable to clearly peer into the future, we must use the information and tools available to us in order to formulate policy.

Policy formation is defined as the systematic development of a plan to meet a need or to act on a problem. It is the first step in the policy process, and the policy analyst or manager must realize that policy formation is very much a political activity. Charles O. Jones (1986) offers six guidelines for policy formulation:

1. Formulation need not be limited to one set of actors. There may be two or more groups producing competing or complementary proposals. Thus, getting one's issue on the agenda is important. Others may not perceive a problem or they may view another problem as more pressing.
2. Formulation may proceed without the problem ever being clearly defined or without formulators ever having much contact with the affected groups.
3. There is no necessary coincidence between formulation and particular institutions, though it is a frequent activity of executive agencies.
4. Formulation and reformulation may occur over a long time without sufficient support for anyone proposal
5. There are often several appeal points for those who lose in the formulation process at anyone level.
6. The process itself is never neutral.

One must also keep in mind that there are at least three different types of policy formation:

- *Routine formation.* This is a repetitive and mostly changeless process of re-formulating similar proposals about an issue. It has a well-established place on the agency, state, or national agenda.
- *Analogous formation.* This refers to treating a new problem by relying on what was done in developing proposals for similar problems in the past.
- *Creative formation.* Creative formation involves developing an essentially unprecedented proposal.

Nearly every type of policy problem will fit one of these types. However, in order to effectively approach policy formation, policy analysts need a framework to help them develop a complete, thorough, and effective policy.

A FRAMEWORK FOR POLICY FORMATION

In chapter 3, we identify the first stage of the policy framework as the input stage which includes formation. In the input stage, all information is brought together to aid the policy analyst or executive in formulating policy that meets the needs of the agency or constituency.

In an another work, Houston (2006) presents a framework for the formation of policy that is adapted from one proposed by Fred R. David (1986). That framework has three stages: the input stage, the matching stage, and the decision stage. The input stage, that is, formulation, is composed of the Internal Factor Evaluation Matrix, the External Factor Evaluation Matrix, and the Other Agency Profile Matrix, which is adapted from David's Competitive Profile Matrix fit well into our notion of policy input.

THE INTERNAL FACTOR EVALUATION MATRIX

The Internal Factor Evaluation (IFE) summarizes the strengths and weaknesses of the organization's key management, public relations, finances, output of services, and planning and research. All factors should be stated objectively. The analyst should keep in mind that a factor can be both a strength and a weakness. If this should occur, the factor should be included twice in the IFE Matrix. An example could be that an organization has an older, experienced management team. The factor can be included as an asset because experience counts a great deal. However, older workers soon retire and often leave a hole in the organization that cannot be easily replaced.

The matrix answers four major questions about an organization (David 1986):

1. What are the organization's key strengths and weaknesses?
2. What is the relative importance of each strength and weakness to the organization's overall performance?
3. Does each factor represent: a major weakness (a rating of 1), a minor weakness (a rating of 2), a minor strength (a rating of 3), or a major strength (a rating of 4).
4. What is the organization's total weighted score resulting from the analysis of the IFE? Is the score above or below 2.50? A score above 2.50 indicates that the organization is favorably positioned for a major policy change.

In establishing the weight for each variable, the formulator uses his or her best judgment. At this particular point, bias is apt to creep into the decision;

Key External Factor	Weight	Rating	Weighted Score
1. Poor management team	.10	4	.40
2. Promising group of young supervisors	.05	3	.15
3. Increasing inmate population	.15	4	.60
4. Few promotional opportunities	.25	4	.75
5. Good employee relations	.25	3	.75
6. Well-kept physical plant	.10	3	.30
7. Poor community relations	.10	1	.10
	1.00		2.35

Figure 7.1.   Internal Factor Evaluation Matrix

thus, we suggest that the weights be arrived at by consensus rather than de-cided upon arbitrarily by one person. The weight score is arrived at by multi-plying across the chart. The sum of all weights cannot exceed 1.00.

THE EXTERNAL FACTOR EVALUATION MATRIX

The second tool available to the analyst or executive for policy formulation is the External Factor Evaluation Matrix (EFE). The EFE is similar to the IFE except that its focus is on the economic, social, cultural, demographic, polit-ical, governmental, legal, and technological opportunities and threats rather than on internal strengths and weaknesses. The analyst first determines the weight of each factor and the weighted score, the same as for the IFE. Figure 7.2 illustrates how this is done. The EFE answers four questions of interest to the analyst or executive (David 1986):

Key External Factor	Weight	Rating	Weighted Score
1. Strong and diversified tax base	.10	4	.40
2. Low unemployment	.05	3	.15
3. Broad community support	.15	4	.60
4. Rising crime rate	.25	4	.75
5. Support of key legislators	.25	3	.75
6. Low prime rate	.10	3	.30
7. Accrediting power threatens to shut down the agency	.10	1	.10
	1.00		3.00

Figure 7.2.   External Factor Evaluation Matrix

1. What are the organization's environmental opportunities and threats?
2. What is the relative importance of each opportunity and threat to the organization's overall performance?
3. Does each factor represent: a major threat (a rating of 1), a minor threat (a rating of 2), a minor opportunity (a rating of 3), or a major opportunity (a rating of 4)?
4. What is the organization's total weighted score on the EFE? Is the score above 2.50? A score greater than 2.50 indicates that the organization is well-positioned for a major policy change.

OTHER AGENCY PROFILE MATRIX

Identifying and analyzing other agencies' strengths, weaknesses, policies/ strategies, and objectives can be a valuable aid to the policy analyst or executive. It could be particularly helpful in private corrections or security when other firms are attempting to penetrate a particular market, or if a public agency is attempting to thwart a private corrections firm's overtures to the legislature, governor, or other elected officials. Therefore, the other agency profile is valuable as an "input" tool that summarizes information about others in the field, or in the case of private corrections, or security, competitors. The Other Agency Profile Matrix (OAPM) probes the following issues:

1. Who are the other agencies/competitors?
2. What key factors are most important to their success in the field of criminal justice?
3. What is the relative importance of each key factor to their success?
4. To what extent is each agency/competitor strong or weak on each of the key factors: a major weakness (a rating of 1), a minor weakness (a rating of 2), a minor strength (a rating of 3), or a major strength (a rating of 4).

As illustrated in figure 7.3, the OAPM usefully summarizes the performance of other agencies/organizations in certain areas. If for any reason information on a public agency is not readily available from staff members, other sources can help, such as government documents. In figure 7.3, we can visualize that the sheriff considering a new jail, and he or she appears to be faced with the politically loaded decision whether to support a private firm for building and managing a new county jail. A score of 3.20 would give some credence to the overtures of Corrections Company of the South.

Key Success Factors	Weight	Muscatine County		Corrections Company of the Midwest		Universal Corrections	
		Rating	Weighted Score	Rating	Weighted Score	Rating	Weighted Score
Service delivery							
Custody	.16	4	.64	4	.64	3	.48
Programs	.09	1	.09	2	.18	1	.09
Food	.16	4	.64	3	.48	3	.48
Health	.12	2	.24	2	.24	2	.24
Per diem cost	.22	4	.88	3	.66	2	.44
Technological ability	.05	1	.05	4	.20	1	.05
Relations with government in other contracts	.13	—	0	4	.52	3	.39
Financial strength	.07	4	.28	4	.28	3	.21
Total Weighted Scores	1.00		2.82		3.20		2.38

Figure 7.3. Other Agency Profile Matrix

THE MATCHING STAGE AND THE TOWS MATRIX

The matching stage is the point at which the analyst or executive can match certain variables in order to devise strategies to overcome identified weaknesses, to take advantage of strengths, or meet identified threats to the organization. The TOWS Matrix allows the analyst to pair internal and external factors to develop strategies for the action or development of policy.

For example, a nonprofit drug rehabilitation center has decided to expand into a neighboring rural county. The county seat is a small, pleasant town where a great deal of pride is taken in the fact that the "problems" of the neighboring big city have not yet arrived, and the citizens aggressively work to thwart the encroachment of "big city" problems. However, they suffer from a severe case of denial relative to the size of the drug problem in the county.

After the analyst from the drug rehabilitation center has prepared an IFE and an EFE, he or she will then develop a TOWS Matrix that draws together the factors from both instruments and match them to devise strategies that overcome weaknesses and take advantage of strengths. Perhaps one strategy would to be to begin an information program via the media that educates the public about the scope and danger of the present use of drugs in the county by youths and adults. The existence of a larger than expected drug-using population would be noted in the opportunity box on the matrix (see figure 7.4), and the ability of the organization to develop a program to meet community needs would be noted in the strengths. Both factors would be matched in the SO Strategies box as "campaign to educate the public."

Matching key internal and external factors requires a good deal of judgment. There is often no best answer; in addition, the purpose is to determine feasible alternatives, not to select the one best way to approach the problem. Thus, we are attempting, through the use of the TOWS Matrix, to make objective, difficult decisions that are based upon often subjective information.

THE DECISION STAGE AND THE QUANTITATIVE STRATEGIC PLANNING MATRIX (QSPM)

At some point, the analyst or the executive needs to make a decision. After gathering sufficient information, the analyst must put it together. The QSPM is a valuable tool for analyzing policy alternatives. The QSPM brings together information from stage 1 and stage 2 to help the analyst objectively decide what alternative to pursue.

(leave blank)	Strengths—S 1. 2. 3. 4. 5. (list strengths) 6. 7. 8. 9. 10.	Weaknesses—W 1. 2. 3. 4. 5. (list weaknesses) 6. 7. 8. 9. 10.
Opportunities—O 1. 2. 3. 4. (list 5. opportunities) 6. 7. 8. 9. 10.	SO Strategies 1. 2. 3. 4. (use strengths to 5. take advantage 6. of opportunities) 7. 8. 9. 10.	WO Strategies 1. 2. 3. 4. (overcome 5. weaknesses by 6. taking advantage 7. of opportunities) 8. 9. 10.
Threats—T 1. 2. 3. 4. (list threats) 5. 6. 7. 8. 9. 10.	ST Strategies 1. 2. 3. 4. (use strengths 5. to avoid threats) 6. 7. 8. 9. 10.	WT Strategies 1. 2. 3. 4. (minimize 5. weaknesses and 6. avoid threats) 7. 8. 9. 10.

Figure 7.4. TOWS Matrix

The format of the QSPM is illustrated in figure 7.5. The key factors column is made up of key internal and key external factors. The top row is comprised of possible alternatives. (Note that the IFE and EFE contribute to the left column.) The next column (rating) is composed of ratings from the IFE and the EFE. The next column is the Attractiveness Score (AS), which is multiplied by the rating to provide the Total Attractiveness Score (TAS). The TAS is then added up to provide a score that when compared to another TAS provides a relative assessment of whether to pursue that particular choice.

Key Factors	Rating	Build New Jail		Renovate Old Jail		Private Corrections Company		Rationale for Attractiveness Score
		AS	TAS	AS	TAS	AS	TAS	
Internal Factors								
Poor management team	1	4	4	1	1	4	4	Coming retirements allow for good people to move up.
Very good public relations	4	4	16	3	12	3	12	
Adequate service image	3	3	9	1	3	3	9	Close-knit community.
No planning or research capability	1	2	2	1	1	4	4	
Stable work force	3	3	9	1	3	3	9	
Good employee relations	3	1	3	1	3	3	9	
Stagnant work force	3	2	6	2	6	2	6	Slow vertical movement.
External Factors								
Rising inmate jail population	1	4	4	1	1	1	1	
$20,000 per month to board prisoners out	1	4	4	1	1	4	4	
Sum total attractiveness score			57		31		58	

Figure 7.5. QSPM

Identifying the organization's key internal strengths and weaknesses and key external threats and opportunities should be relatively easy when the IFE and EFE Matrices are reviewed. One also assigns ratings to the key factors as listed on the IFE and EFE. By reviewing the TOWS Matrix, one can identify possible alternatives. Determining this involves simply attaching the numerical score of I to 4 (not acceptable to most acceptable). One then simply computes the TAS and adds up the scores for an indication of which direction to pursue.

LIMITATIONS OF POLICY FORMATION

The major limitation of the framework is that the subjective ratings allow bias to creep into the process. Bias can be used by the policy maker, executive, or analyst to justify (or fail to justify) a major decision. Therefore, an analyst must constantly be on guard against personal bias as well as the bias of subordinates.

Another issue is time. If the analyst or executive has a planning department that can devote time to gathering information and devising alternative courses of action, the framework is well worth the effort. However, in smaller agencies where there is no planning department and the planning function is left up to the agency head, the framework may prove to be cumbersome and time consuming. In addition, there also may not be many variables to consider in any given policy decision. In that instance, the agency head may use the QSPM alone as a strategic tool without doing much more than simply penciling out the variables to be considered.

PITFALLS OF THE POLICY PROCESS

The policy process is highly interactive, and the analyst or executive must recognize that he or she works in an interactive world and cannot ignore the interactions between participants and their values and resource environment (Brewer and deLeon 1983). Thus, a major pitfall of the policy process is that proceeding without consideration of the interactions between actors, values, and politics may doom any policy initiative from the start.

Brewer and deLeon (1983) point out that policy is bounded by threats and resources that have three components: (1) criteria used to define the problem, (2) relevant contextual or environmental parameters, and (3) proper time constraints. Selection of the criteria is important and functional to the process. Therefore, one must ask the proper questions in order to determine the problem criteria and be able to recognize the proper answers, thereby being able to describe the problem with some precision to others. In addition, according to Brewer and deLeon, the lack of proper criteria will introduce error in the selection of the proper policy alternatives. Determining the relevant contextual or environmental parameters is important in that one must understand how the problem fits into the general organizational environment. If the analyst is unable to do so, he or she will be unable to anticipate how the various actors will interact.

Determining the proper time constraints is important because one must understand how much time will pass before the problem begins to have adverse affects. Urgent problems create deadlines and deadlines create a greater probability for mistakes. Finally, bias is a problem in the policy process in that the analyst must consistently be on guard to prevent bias from creeping into his or her judgments and therefore skew the formation and implementation of policy. Bias can best be prevented by including subordinates and colleagues in the process. Lively debate will help the analyst arrive at the best judgments possible.

SUMMARY

Clearly, criminal justice policy analysts must be able to muster a variety of tools and information to formulate and analyze policy. However, all too often the policy process in criminal justice is conducted haphazardly by legislators and public servants who are not well grounded in the techniques and art of policy analysis.

Criminal justice analysts must be equipped with a wealth of information about crime patterns, crime causation, and key factors in the development of criminal careers. Criminal justice policy analysts must have an in-depth knowledge about the machinery of criminal justice, and must be thoroughly familiar with policy analysis and planning tools.

Information to aid the policy analyst is available from a variety of sources, including the organizational management information system (MIS); organizational records and personnel, inmate/probationers/parolees; the local university and public library; and local, state, regional, and national private sources.

Planning the workload and approach to the policy process requires the rational organization of data and information. The Gantt Chart and PERT offer valuable ways to organize the workload and tasks of planners and analysts. The objective is to formulate and implement policy in a way that best meets the needs of taxpayers and the organization. While some precision is lost, the use of statistics is the best way to present a great deal of information in a meaningful way and still make the information understandable to the average person.

The Internal Factor Evaluation Matrix, the External Factor Evaluation Matrix, the Other Agency Profile, and the Quantitative Strategic Planning Matrix are valuable tools that organize information gleaned from the internal and external environment. The information can then be used to render as objective a judgment as possible for the formulation of policy.

REVIEW QUESTIONS

1. Define a management information system. Why is an MIS valuable to the policy analyst?
2. In planning for policy formation, what kinds of data are available and where can we get that information?
3. What do the Internal Factor Evaluation Matrix and the External Factor Evaluation Matrix do for you as a planner?
4. What is a QSPM? Why is it important?

Chapter Eight

Improving Crime Policy in Theory and Practice

INTRODUCTION

Revisiting the Liberal/Conservative Debate

Some political leaders call for more police, more prosecutions, and more incarcerations. The question that ought to be addressed is, "Just how many more police and prisons are the taxpayers willing to support?" Additionally, how far are citizens willing to allow their civil liberties to be eroded to bring about a crackdown on crime? Those who support the "get tough" philosophy view the strategy as a deterrent as well as a vehicle for more severe punishment. The strategy holds that actual instances of crime will drop as would-be criminals rethink their action knowing harsh consequences will surely follow. Unfortunately, humans are not that predictable. In practice, societies with the lowest reported crime rates also tend to have the fewest individual freedoms. In addition, most American experts agree that in the United States, there is neither the money to continue to build more prisons nor the desire to give up freedoms for the punishment strategy to be successful.

It is interesting to note that in conservative camps, it is inappropriate to compare the United States with other countries on social issues so important to liberals. Socialism is not the American way, and the last thing we need, conservatives argue, is national health care, a ban on guns, and more government. Yet, this same conservative movement is pro-government when dealing with crime, and in this instance points to foreign success stories. The solution to crime, they assert, is more spending and greater government intervention. In this vein, it is interesting to note that China has a very low reported crime rate. Can we learn much from their form of government? Americans also must realize that conservatives, at least with respect to crime, are in favor of more, not less, government. That is, more governmental suppression, directly or indirectly.

The alternatives presented by the political left emphasize prevention. The prevention strategy can only work if the program is well grounded in theory. Unfortunately, liberals have, for the most part, poorly understood causality. In the past, Democrats have treated crime as a function of poverty, economics, and minority struggles. As James Q. Wilson correctly states, "There are many poor men of all races who do not abandon the woman they have impregnated and many poor women of all races who avoid drugs and do a good job of raising their children. If we fail to stigmatize those who give way to temptations, we withdraw the rewards from those who resist them" (Wilson and Petersilia, 1995). Likewise, most youths in depressed neighborhoods are able to walk away from delinquency and eventually lead law-abiding lives. Indeed, liberals and conservatives must come to grips with the notion that there is no silver bullet in the fight against crime, and understand that suppression, opportunity, and prevention programs must share the stage.

Further, both liberal and conservative thinkers shudder when confronted with balancing individual rights with societal beliefs and values. Nowhere is this more apparent than in the debate over the fate of convicted murderer Karla Faye Tucker. Found guilty in a Texas court of committing murder with a pickaxe during a robbery, Tucker appeared to be an obvious candidate for the death penalty. However, between the time of her conviction and execution, some conservatives noted her conversion to Christianity and sought to stay the execution. Additionally, conservative ideologues are more paternalistic towards women and thus believe they should be treated more gently than men. Appeals of the *Tucker* verdict proved unsuccessful, culminating with the U.S. Supreme Court's refusal to stay the execution. In contrast, liberals who typically oppose the death penalty argue that gender equity requires equal treatment under the law, hence justifying the death sentence. The case demonstrates that liberal or conservative ideology is easy to profess in the abstract but difficult to apply in the real world. There is room for liberal and conservative thought in crime policy, but we challenge criminal justice analysts, legislators, and practitioners to push the debate towards the pragmatic. For it is only through hard work, research, and reasoned debate, not rhetoric, that effective crime policy can be formulated.

COMING TO GRIPS WITH THE ROOT CAUSES OF CRIME

There is an abundance of evidence that points to personality, early family experiences, and neighborhood effects as the major causes of street crime (Wilson and Petersilia, 1995). Both Democrats and Republicans have come to recognize the importance of these contributing factors. Unfortunately, both parties have opted to interpret these causes as confirmation of their particular political philosophies rather than to devise new and innovative strategies for dealing with the crime problem. The most apparent strategy of recent years has been the attempt by both parties to corner the market on family values. Democrats argue the need for more social programs, and Republicans lobby for elimination of social programs, which they claim encourage family breakup. These positions are not new, and, in fact, are a common focus of debate between contemporary Democrats and Republicans. There are precious few new ideas in either approach.

What should be done about children raised by parent(s) with a criminal past, or children who experience poor parental supervision? Experimental preschool/ parental training programs in large urban area "at risk" neighborhoods have demonstrated improved self-control among participants. The programs included workable teacher-child caseloads, extensive home visits, and elaborate parent training (Wilson and Petersilia, 1995), but it is doubtful that such programs can be molded into an effective national policy. Head Start is held in high esteem among liberals, and originally included the very elements included in the early intervention experiments. Initially, Head Start was expanded quickly, but because of budget restraints was quickly watered down to provide only for a pre-school education (Wilson and Petersilia, 1995).

FINDING THE MONEY AND DECIDING WHERE TO SPEND IT

Combined with today's ever-tightening budget, Republican control of Congress, and a nationwide distrust of government, it is unlikely that early crime intervention programs will become a national policy. Efforts in early intervention seem destined to become (or remain) the purview of state and local government. At present, the National Institute of Justice provides some general guidelines and grant funds to support local experiments, but early intervention on a grand scale is quite unlikely at this point. Returning power to the states through block grants was also politically popular in the nineties, but it came with a cost; we need only remember the abuses of Law Enforcement Assistance Administration (LEAA) money in the 1970s when state plans became nothing more than wish lists for chiefs of police. There is likely to be little uniformity in the programs if there is little control from Washington, D.C., and areas will differ greatly regarding the level of funding (if any) as well as political commitment to these sorts of projects. On a positive note, the diversity of state and local government structures allows for experiments that are fine-tuned to meet the needs of a particular area.

Despite policy innovation a the state level, a basic question waiting to be answered regarding the crime issue is whether the American public is willing to make the commitment necessary to reduce crime? Whether the public ultimately decides to opt for the conservative or liberal approach, or a combination thereof, a greater commitment will be required in funding and in terms of governmental intervention. These two factors, however, are not presently popular. Since Ronald Reagan was elected with the mandate that government is the problem, the past twenty-five years has seen few instances where the public thought government could do anything right or that (in domestic matters) the taxpayer's contributions were funds well spent.

On the surface, the public appears willing to entertain the idea that government can do more in combating crime. But beneath the surface, there lurks attitudes spawned by the Reagan legacy: citizens distrust law enforcement, especially federal law enforcement agencies; police, for the most part, are no more than an extension of big government and the heavy hand of authority, and when left unchecked become almost tyrannical in nature. Deficit reduction is also a priority. National efforts to balance the budget not only limit Washington's ability to fund crime programs but also impacts state and local efforts. The specter of the Patriot Act further exacerbates these complex attitudes toward crime.

As federal grants become even more scarce, states are challenged to pick up the tab. Most states and localities today also face budget restrictions (that is, state constitutional amendments to balance budgets). Additionally, the Tenth Amendment to the Constitution gives primary responsibility of law enforcement to the states. So, most states already have allocated their budgets to the fullest extent simply to implement existing crime policies. Thus, the fiscal challenge is one of meeting public demand to do something about crime in a political environment where significant revenue enhancement is highly improbable.

One note is necessary here to explain why so many states are in budgetary trouble. For many decades, the Federal government and the state governments played an elaborate shell game. The states were allowed to keep state income taxes low and the Federal government had a much higher income tax rate. This was politically popular and allowed local and state politicians to point out that they were against higher taxes. In return, however, the states and local governments received block grants and other "pass through" money from the federal government. Problems began when a Republican Congress made good on lower taxes. The resultant tax reductions meant less money for the states and local governments which traditionally have been reluctant to raise taxes. The consequences have been a reduction in services and cries from the public that something ought to be done; just don't raise taxes.

CIVIL LIBERTIES IN FLUX

Analysis of how to cope with crime would not be complete without commenting on the constitutional dilemma between freedom and security. After 9/11 this balance became the sine qua non of public government action. The debate is a semi-permanent. Domestic terrorism such as the Oklahoma City bombing of the federal building and the pipe bomb explosion at Olympic Park during the 1996 Atlanta Summer Olympics brought the issue to the foreground. Terrorism from foreign enemies have made freedom the ultimate struggle for government, yet history tells us that Americans tend to be short term in their willingness to give up personal freedoms or rights in return for greater personal security. While never entirely complacent, there is a desire to get back to a state of normalcy. The World Trade Center attacks and Oklahoma City bombings both heightened security concerns that are diminishing. Clearly, the public is willing to put up with extraordinary measures in the short term or in a crisis situation.

There is no evidence to support the notion that over an extended period (or permanently, for that matter), the public is willing to give up basic rights and liberties guaranteed in the Bill of Rights. Justice could be more swift and certain, but it would require direct challenges to guaranteed rights such as that of trial by jury, defense, appeals, protection from unreasonable searches, and protection against self-incrimination (Wilson and Petersilia, 1995). While a more conservative Supreme Court is willing to entertain exceptions to rights and liberties, the only swift and sure way to prosecute and convict is to overturn the Bill of Rights. Thus, analysis of crime policy reveals a judicial, legal, and legislative process that attempts to strike a balance between extremes. Nobody would ever suggest that a lawless society would solve the crime problem, although hypothetically, in a lawless society there can be no crime since there are no laws to be broken. At the other extreme, it is unrealistic to expect Americans to willingly and enthusiastically give up the very freedoms on which they believe the country to be founded.

In the United States, there is a delicate balancing act between coping with crime and protecting freedoms. Nearly every American has broken the law in one form or another. A drive down the road in an automobile is all one has to do to observe this fact. Yet, one does not encounter a standing-room only line of volunteer offenders at the police station to pay self-assessed traffic violation fines. As noted previously in this text, we are becoming a more litigious society (not judging merit, but caseloads), and every year more and more activities are made illegal than are legalized. Thus, the question remains: are Americans willing to give up even more freedom for a more security minded (police-state) society? It seems unlikely

PROSPECTS AND LIMITATIONS OF THE POLICY CYCLE

Examination of the crime issue through the lens of the policy cycle reveals that policy evolves in a continuous loop. Policy in general is incremental, with periodic adjustment to correct for past errors and political trends. Crime policy illustrates quite well the nature of the political process. Policy evaluation, for instance, reveals that most crime measures are more "feel good" measures than direct assaults on the root causes of crime. The errors noted in the Patriot Act are mostly a reflection of popular political trends and philosophies. Precious little in the response to terrorism is based on scientific cause and effect methodology.

The policy cycle provides a solid foundation from which crime policy students and practitioners can build in developing more sophisticated and issue-specific frameworks for analysis. Several of the more scientific research techniques are presented in Part Three of this text (a general critique of these research models appears a bit later in this chapter). It is essential for students and practitioners of a specific field of study, such as criminal justice, to become well grounded in the politics, process, and history of an issue, and not simply react to issues, technical points, and administrative aspects. The policy cycle provides an easily understood, well-organized, and widely accepted analytical tool to develop an adequate background on any issue, including crime.

The policy cycle provides avenues for finding more information about the causes, content, and consequences of public policies. At the same time, policy students learn more about the institutions, processes, and politics at work in government. Knowing what government does helps determine what is expected of officeholders and in turn how they behave (Anderson, 1994). Further, criminal justice practitioners can become better prepared and skilled when dealing with political actors through the study of the policy cycle.

The policy cycle, as with any means of inquiry, is not without its flaws. The macro-level approach precludes specific analyses targeted for specific instances or problems. The individual tends to be diminished in favor of observance of institutional behaviors, trends, and aggregate conclusions about how things ought to work. Rational choice theory, in many respects, can be viewed as the antithesis of the policy cycle approach. If a researcher is interested in how a particular actor makes and reaches a decision, then rational choice theory provides for a more appropriate level of analysis. Still another criticism leveled against the policy cycle approach is that the technique is so broad that at some point everything explains everything. This is a criticism that is also made of systems theory. Further, just as systems theory is criticized for claiming to be value neutral, so too can the same critique be made of the policy cycle approach (Susser, 1996).

Certainly, if one does not start with an open mind, it is very easy to use the policy cycle as a way of reinforcing preconceptions about the world. Additionally, the policy cycle when viewed as a systems approach can be challenged as too generic to be useful. The policy cycle "might simply be called a restatement of the essential elements in the political process stripped bare of any and all specific characteristics, a minimalistic conceptualization that gains clarity at the price of abstraction" (Susser, 1996).

In the final analysis, the macro-level approach developed in Part Two of this text can be a worthwhile endeavor. Just as it would seem unthinkable to allow someone to claim to be a general medical practitioner if he or she did not have a general understanding of subjects such as medicine, biology and chemistry, students of crime policy should take the time to gain a better understanding of public policy, politics, and institutions. The policy cycle approach offered here provides a step-by-step process for developing a background and feel for the environment that criminal justice students and practitioners will routinely encounter. More sophisticated approaches to policy analysis can be introduced and mastered down the road. For the newcomer to the policy arena and the crime issue, the policy cycle offers some guidelines and parameters and perhaps a little order to an environment that might at first glance appear chaotic.

PROMISES AND PITFALLS OF POLICY ANALYSIS

While local control of polices and procedures are of the utmost importance, even more important is the input of criminal justice practitioners at all levels on the policy and legislative process, whether at the level of the courthouse, the state legislature, or Congress. Legislation and policy are frequently formulated based upon hysteria and poor information, and legislators pay no attention to the unanticipated consequences of the policy. Leaders in criminal justice can have an impact if they are aware of the policy process and understand the dynamics of agenda setting, formulation, legitimization, and implementation. The consequences of the failure of practitioners to participate aggressively in the process are all too clear—they are forced to implement poorly written and ill-conceived legislation and policy, and often take the heat when the process goes awry.

The task for managers and executives is to be familiar with the principles of management and the etiology of criminal behavior so that they can sufficiently impress upon elected officials the linkage between theory and policy. However, we must be willing to pay a price if we profess to be interested in the public good. If elected officials are interested in serving the public good, they also must pay a price; that is, it is important that legislation and policy be linked to causation. We must pay the price of giving up cherished myths.

CONCLUDING THOUGHTS

Most of the literature on crime and what to do about it projects a rather bleak picture. As pointed out in this text, there are both political and scientific remedies that may reduce crime. Scholars, however, tend to conclude that the country lacks the will to address the root causes of crime (Wilson and Petersilia, 1995). A lack of money and a resistance to limiting freedoms appear to be the major hurdles standing in the way of progress. Politics as usual also appears entrenched. The debate seems centered on peripheral issues such as the death penalty or violence on television while solutions tend to be trendy and promise much at very cheap prices (Wilson and Petersilia, 1995). While this text recognizes the misgivings of the critics of crime policy, the policy cycle approach does not necessarily lock one into thinking the future is bleak and hopeless.

Policy analysis is not a panacea for positive change. Done properly, policy research not only unlocks the door to problems but also offers a roadmap for producing effective and positive results. Some of the frustration regarding violent crime, for example, is no doubt related to the fact that the impact of violence is sudden and swift, whereas government responds to the perpetrators of the act so slowly.

It is easy to conclude in today's fast-paced and cyber-highway society that incrementalism is a symptom of governmental failure. The policy cycle approach presented in this text reveals that incremental change is exactly what the framers of the Constitution had in mind when they created the government of the United States, and this approach is emulated by nearly all states. It is next to impossible for radical ideas to be passed into law by elected officials. About the only avenue for radical change is a constitutional amendment, in itself a long and drawn-out process. The strength of the incremental approach is its ability to expose and prevent the implementation of bad ideas.

Another benefit of the policy cycle approach is that it puts the goals of public policy into perspective. Current methodology is better at correcting past errors than it is at solving problems in the future. No matter how sophisticated, society still has not developed a crystal ball that predicts outcomes and projects solutions to problems. Policy analysis is about finding the hits and misses of previous policies, making adjustments, and then observing the results of the changes. For those who want a quick fix, or whose ideology tells them that there is only one solution, policy analysis is a waste of time, and government can only be seen as a failed experiment.

The policy cycle approach reveals that doing a little bit with the goal of making some progress over the long haul is certainly better than immediate surrender. Correcting errors and incremental change is certainly a safer and better calculated course than acting on a whim. The policy cycle approach also assists the researcher in developing specific research topics. More research is needed in the criminal justice field with respect to agenda setting, government action, implementation, and policy evaluation. Research opportunities exist at the national, state, and local levels.

Recently passed legislation at both the state and local levels offers ample opportunity to assess the impact of crime-control options. For instance, many states have passed laws permitting citizens to carry concealed weapons as a deterrent to street crime. Further research is also needed to evaluate the various "Brady Bill"-type laws that have been implemented at the state level. From the prevention side, crime policy analysts need to continue to search for definitive correlations that point to the root causes of criminal behavior and for effective intervention strategies that turn individuals (especially youth) away from trouble.

Is crime a problem? On the one hand, as long as one criminal exists, someone will correctly argue that it is a problem. If government, and society for that matter, is to be judged by the absence of crime, then we have failed and always may fail. Research indicates that 6 percent of the members of society are destined to be criminals (Wilson and Petersilia, 1995). This conclusion suggests that the elimination of crime may be an unrealistic goal.

On the other hand, given that we live in a free and more open society, control of crime indeed may be a realistic goal. Today's concerns stem not so much from the total number of crimes, but the types of crimes citizens fear most: drive by-shootings, random violence, gangs, and drugs. If this is what is truly on the minds of the public, then a crime policy that deals with only the peripheral, and stresses containment rather than elimination, ought to be viewed as appropriate.

Policies that deal with the visible aspects of crime will not stop crime, but they might make the average citizen feel better about living in an open society.

Government should not be blamed for failing to implement a crime-elimination policy that would require the public to give up more in taxes, rights, and liberties (issues that the public finds more important than crime). Government cannot be judged as a failure regarding crime policy when its representatives are offering exactly what the public demands on this issue.

Finally, to students and criminal justice practitioners, policy analysis is merely a tool to assist in decision-making. The goal of this text is to introduce students of crime policy to tools and techniques that can improve their understanding of the crime issue and to work more effectively with officials of government at all levels. Crime policy can only improve through commitment and dedication. Change will not happen overnight and frustration can be replaced with constructive work. The shortcomings of the political process need to be understood and worked with, not condemned. The challenge is to work in the field and work towards improvement, not to give up in disgust or rationalize that little or nothing can be accomplished.

Bibliography

CHAPTER 1: OVERVIEW OF PUBLIC POLICY ANALYSIS

Anderson, James E. 1997. *Public Policymaking: An Introduction*, 3d ed. Boston Houghton Mifflin.

Certo, Samuel C. 1985. *Principles of Modern Management*, 3d ed. Dubuque, Iowa: William C. Brown.

Dahl, Robert A. 1961. *Who Governs: Democracy and Power in an American City.* New Haven, Connecticut: Yale University Press.

Dye, Thomas R. 2002. *Top Down Policy Making.* New York: Chatham House.

Easton, David. 1979a. *A Framework for Political Analysis.* Chicago, Illinois: Universityof Chicago Press.

Easton, David. 1979b. *A Systems Analysis of Political Life.* Chicago, Illinois: University\of Chicago Press.

Gimpel, James. 1996. *Fulfilling the Contract: The First One Hundred Days.* Boston, Massachusetts: Allyn and Bacon.

Hill, Michael, and Peter Hupe. 2002. *Implementing Public Policy: Governance in Theory and in Practice.* Thousand Oaks, CA: Sage Publications

Jones, Charles O. 1984. *An Introduction to the Study of Public Policy.* 3d ed. Pacific Grove, California: Brooks/Cole.

Lindblom, Charles. 1959. The Science of Muddling Through. *Public Administration Review 19.*

Lindbloom, Charles, and Edward J. Woodhouse. 1993. *The Policy-Making Process,* 3d ed. Englewood Cliffs, New Jersey: Prentice-Hall.

Mood, Alexander. 1983. *Introduction to Policy Analysis.* New York: North-Holland.

Pressman, Jeffrey L., and Aaron B. Wildavsky. 1973. *Implementation.* Berkeley, California: University of California Press.

Ripley, Randall B. 1984. *Policy Analysis in Political Science.* Chicago, Illinois: Nelson-Hall.

Susser, Bernard. 1992. *Approaches to the Study of Politics.* New York: Macmillan.
Walker, Samuel. 1994. *Sense and Nonsense about Crime and Drugs,* 3d ed. Belmont, California: Wadsworth.
Wildavsky, Aaron. 1979. *Speaking Truth to Power: The Art and Craft of Policy Analysis.* Boston, Massachusetts: Little, Brown.
Wilson, James Q. 1983. *Thinking about Crime.* New York: Basic Books.

CHAPTER 2: INFLUENCES ON CRIMINAL JUSTICE POLICY

Bachrach, Peter and Morton S. Baratz. 1970. *Power and Poverty: Theory and Practice.* New York: Oxford University Press.
Bennett, W. Lance. 1996. *The Governing Crisis.* New York: St. Martin's Press.
Buchanan, James M. 1984. *The Theory of Public Choice II.* Ann Arbor: University of Michigan Press.
Dahl, Robert A. 1967. *Pluralist Democracy in the United States: Conflict and Consensus.* Chicago, Illinois: Rand McNally.
Dionne, E. J. 1991. *Why Americans Hate Politics.* New York: Simon and Schuster.
Downs, Anthony. 1972. Up and Down with Ecology: The Issue Attention Cycle. *Public Interest* 32 (Summer).
Dye, Thomas R. 1995. *The Irony of Democracy: An Uncommon Introduction to American Politics.* San Diego, California: Harcourt, Brace.
Dye, Thomas R. 2002. *Top Down Policymaking.* New York: Chatham House.
Edelman, Murray. 1985. The Symbolic Uses of Politics. Champaign: University of Illinois Press.
Fiorina, Morris. 1996. *Divided Government,* 2d ed. Boston, Massachusetts: Allyn and Bacon.
Gimpel, James. 1996. *Fulfilling the Contract: The First 100 Days.* Boston, Massachusetts: Allyn and Bacon.
Goldberg, Bernard. 2002. *Bias: A CBS Insider Exposes How the Media Distorts the News.* Washington, DC: Regnery Publishing Co.
Gwartney, James D. 1994. *Economics: Private and Public Choice.* Orlando, Florida: Dryden Press.
Hardon, Garret. 1968. The Tragedy of the Commons. *Science* 162: 1243.
Henry, Nicholas. 1995. *Public Administration,* 6th ed. Englewood Cliffs, New Jersey: Prentice-Hall.
Johnson, Haynes, and David S. Broder. 1996. *The System: The American Way of Politics at the Breaking Point.* Boston, Massachusetts: Little, Brown.
King, Dennis. 1989. *Lyndon LaRouche and the New American Fascism.* New York: Doubleday.
Lowi, Theodore. 1979. *The End of Liberalism.* New York: Norton.
Olson, Mancur, Jr. 1971. *The Logic of Collective Action: Public Goods and the Theory of Goods.* Cambridge, Massachusetts: Harvard University Press.

Quirk, Paul and Joseph Hinchcliffe. 1996. Domestic Policy: The Trials of a Centrist Democrat. In Colin Campbell and Bert Rockman, eds., *The Clinton Presidency: First Appraisals.* Chatham, New Jersey: Chatham House.

Rappaport, Annatol. 1960. *Fights, Games, and Debates.* Ann Arbor: University of Michigan Press.

Schattschneider, E. E. 1975. *The Semi-Sovereign People.* Orlando, Florida.: Harcourt, Brace.

Shorenstein Center. 2005. The Joan Shorenstein Center on the Press, Politics, and Public Policy (2000). Doing Well and Doing Good: How Soft News and Critical Journalism are Shrinking the News Audience and Weakening Democracy– And What News Outlets Can Do about it. Thomas Patterson. Located at http:// ksgnotes1.harvard.edu/research/wpaper.nsf/rwp/RWP01-001/$File/rwp01_001 _patterson.pdf

Wilcox, Clyde. 1995. *The Latest American Revolution?* New York: St. Martin's Press.

Wildavsky, Aaron. 1979. *Speaking Truth to Power: The Art and Craft of Policy Analysis.* Boston: Little, Brown.

Wright, John R. 1996. *Interest Groups and Congress: Lobbying, Contributions, and Influence.* Boston, Massachusetts: Allyn and Bacon.

CHAPTER 3: HOW CRIME POLICY IS MADE

Anderson, James E. 1997. *Public Policy Making: An Introduction,* 3d ed. Boston, Massachusetts: Houghton Mifflin.

Bachrach, Peter and Morton S. Baratz. 1970. *Power and Poverty: Theory and Practice.* New York: Oxford University Press.

Bonser, Charles F., Eugene B. McGregor, and Clinton V. Oster. 1996. *Policy Choices and Public Action.* Englewood Cliffs, New Jersey: Prentice-Hall.

Brewer, Gary D., and Peter de Leon. 1983. *Foundations of Policy Analysis.* Chicago, Illinois: Dorsey Press.

Campbell, Colin, and Bert Rockman, eds. 1996. *The Clinton Presidency: First Appraisals.* Englewood Cliffs, New Jersey: Prentice-Hall.

Cobb, Roger W., and Charles D. Elder. 1983. *Participation in American Politics: The Dynamics of Agenda Building,* 2d ed. Baltimore, Maryland: Johns Hopkins University Press.

Davidson, Roger and Walter Oleszek. 1981. *Congress and Its Members.* Washington, DC: CQ Press.

Easton, David A. 1979. *A Systems Analysis of Political Life.* Chicago, Illinois: University of Chicago Press.

Fiorina, Morris. 1996. *Divided Government,* 2d ed. Boston, Massachusetts: Allyn and Bacon.

Frantzich, Stephen E. and Steven E. Shier. 1995. *Congress: Games and Strategies.* Dubuque, Iowa: Brown and Benchmark.

Gallup Opinion Polls, Various Years Archived at www.gallup.com

Goggin, Malcolm, James Lester, and Laurence O'Toole. 1990. *Implementation Theory and Practice: Toward a Third Generation.* Reading, Pennsylvania: Addison-Wesley.

Heclo, Hugh. 1978. Issue Networks and the Executive Establishment. In Anthony King, ed., *The New American Political System.* Washington, DC: American Enterprise Institute for Public Policy Research.

Henry, Nicholas. 1995. *Public Administration.* 6th ed. Englewood Cliffs, New Jersey: Prentice-Hall.

Ingram, Helen. 1987. Implementation: A Review and Suggested Framework. In Aaron Wildavsky and Naomi Lynn, eds., *Public Administration: The State of the Discipline.* Chatham, New Jersey: Chatham House.

Johnson, Haynes and David S. Broder. 1996. *The System: The American Way of Politics at the Breaking Point.* Boston, Massachusetts: Little, Brown.

Jones, Charles O. 1984. *An Introduction to the Study of Public Policy,* 3d ed. Pacific Grove, California: Brooks/Cole.

Kingdon, John W. 1995. *Agendas, Alternatives, and Public Policies,* 2d ed. New York: HarperCollins.

Lester, James P. and Joseph Stewart. 1996. *Public Policy: An Evolutionary Approach.* St. Paul, Minnesota: West.

Lindblom, Charles E. 1959. The Science of "Muddling Through." *Public Administration Review* 19 (Spring): 79–88.

Mazmanian, Daniel and Paul Sabatier. 1983. *Implementation and Public Policy.* Glenview, Illinois: Scott Forsman.

Neustadt, Richard E. 1990. *Presidential Power and the Modern Presidents.* New York: Free Press.

O'Brien, David M. 1990. *Storm Center: The Supreme Court in American Politics,* 2d ed. New York: Free Press.

Pressman, Jeffrey L. and Aaron Wildavsky. 1973. *Implementation.* Berkeley: University of California Press.

Rothwax, Harold. 1997. *Guilty: The Collapse of the Criminal Justice System*, Warner Books: NY

Smith, Hedrick. 1988. *The Power Game.* New York: Ballantine.

Spitzer, Robert J. 1995. *The Politics of Gun Control.* Chatham, New Jersey: Chatham House.

Stillman, Richard J. 1996. *Public Administration,* 6th ed. Boston, Massachusetts: Houghton-Mifflin.

Van Meter, Donald and Carl Van Horn. 1975. The Policy Implementation Process: A Conceptual Framework. *Administration and Society 6.*

Wayne, Stephen 1. *The Road to the White House* 1996: *The Politics of Presidential Elections.* New York: St. Martin's Press.

Wildavsky, Aaron. 1979. *Speaking Truth to Power: The Art and Craft of Policy Analysis.* Boston, Massachusetts: Little, Brown.

CHAPTER 4: THE POLICY CYCLE APPLIED
TO THE CRIME ISSUE

Anderson, James E. 1997. *Public Policymaking: An Introduction,* 3d ed. Boston: Houghton Mifflin.

Berman, Larry, and Emily Goldman. 1996. Clinton's Foreign Policy at Midterm. In Colin Campbell, and Bert Rockman, eds., *The Clinton Presidency: First Appraisals.* Chatham, New Jersey: Chatham House.

Bonser, Charles E, Eugene B. McGregor, and Clinton V. Oster. 1996. *Policy Choices and Public Action.* Upper Saddle River, New Jersey: Prentice-Hall.

Clear, Todd and George Cole, 2000. *American Corrections.* Belmont, CA: Wadsworth

Cochran, Clarke E., T. R. Carr, Lawrence C. Mayer, and N. Joseph Cayer. 1996. *American Public Policy: An Introduction.* New York: St. Martin's Press.

Cohen, Stanley (1972): *Folk Devils and Moral Panics* London: MacGibbon and Kee *Commission on Safety and Abuse in America's Prisons. 2006.*

Congressional Quarterly Weekly Report. 1994. May 7.

Dionne, E. J. 1991. *Why Americans Hate Politics.* New York: Simon and Schuster.

Edwards, George C. III, and Stephen J. Wayne. 2005. *Presidential Leadership: Politics and Politics Making.* New York: St. Martin's Press.

Erikson, Robert and Kent Tedin. 2002. American Public Opinion: Its Origin, Contents, and Impact, Update Edition, 6th Ed. New York: Longman.

Federal Bureau of Investigation. www.fbi.gov

Flanagan, Timothy J. and Dennis R. Longmire, eds. 1996. *Americans View Crime and Justice: A National Public Opinion Survey.* Thousand Oaks, California: Sage.

Gordon, George J. and Michael E. Milokovich. 1995. *Public Administration in America,* 5th ed. New York: St. Martin's Press.

Jones, Charles O. 1996. Campaigning to Govern. In Colin Campbell and Bert Rockman, eds., *The Clinton Presidency: First Appraisals.* Chatham, New Jersey: Chatham House.

Langan, Patrick & Levin, David. 2002. Recidivism of Prisoners Released in 1994. Bureau of Justice Statistics. U.S. Department of Justice

Leone, Richard C. and Greg Anrig, Jr., eds. 2003. *The War on Our Freedoms: Civil Liberties in an Age of Terrorism.* New York: The Century Foundation.

Lester, James P. and Joseph J. Stewart. 1996. *Public Policy: An Evolutionary Approach.* St. Paul, Minnesota: West.

Lindblom, Charles. 1959. The Science of Muddling Through. *Public Administration Review. 19* (Summer).

Lindblom, Charles and Edward J. Woodhouse. 1993. The Policy Making Process, 3rd ed. Englewood Cliffs, New Jersey: Prentice Hall.

Marion, Nancy E. 1995. *A Primer in the Politics of Criminal Justice.* New York: Harrow and Heston.

Martinson, Robert. 1974.What Works? - Questions and Answers About Prison Reform, *The Public Interest,* 35: 22–54

Mendelberg, Tali. 1997 Tali Executing Hortons: Racial Crime in the 1988 Presidential Campaign. *The Public Opinion Quarterly*, Vol. 61, No. 1, Special Issue on Race. pp. 134–157

Morris, Norvill and Michael Tonry. 1991. *Between Prison and Probation: Intermediate Punishments in a Rational Sentencing System.* Oxford Press.

National Institute of Corrections www.nicic.gov

Neimi, Richard G., John Mueller, and Tom W. Smith. 1989. *Trends in Public Opinion: A Compendium of Survey Data.* New York: Greenwood.

Office of Victims of Crime http://www.ojp.usdoj.gov/ovc/

Packer, Herb. 1968. The Limits of the Criminal Sanction, Stanford University Press

Quirk, Paul and Joseph Hinchcliffe. 1996. Domestic Policy: The Trials of a Centrist Democrat. In Colin Campbell and Bert Rockman, eds., *The Clinton Presidency: First Appraisals.* Chatham, New Jersey: Chatham House.

Schmallager, Frank. 2005. *Criminal Justice Today,* 6th edition. Upper Saddle River, New Jersey: Prentice Hall.

Sherman, Laurence W. and David Weisbard. 1995. General Deterrent Effects of Police Patrol in Crime "Hot Spots." *Justice Quarterly 12(4).*

Sabato, Larry. 1987. Real and Imagined Corruption in Campaign Financing. In A. James Reichley, ed., *Elections American Style.* Washington, DC: Brookings Institution.

United States Sentencing Commission www.ussc.gov

Wilson, James Q., and Richard J. Hermstein. 1985. *Crime and Human Nature.* New York: Simon and Schuster.

CHAPTER 5: MISSION STATEMENTS AND POLICIES AND PROCEDURES

Georgia Department of Corrections www.dcor.state.ga.us/

Bozeman, Glenn and Arvind Phatak. 1989. *Strategic Management: Text and Cases,* 2d ed. New York: Wiley.

Certo, Samuel C. 1985. *Principles of Modern Management: Functions and Systems,* 3d ed. Dubuque, Iowa: Wm. C. Brown.

Commission on Accreditation for Law Enforcement Agencies, Inc. *Standards for Law Enforcement Agencies: The Standards Manual of the Law Enforcement Agency Accreditation Program.* Fairfax, VA: N.p., 1989.

David, Fred R. 1986. *Fundamentals of Strategic Management.* Columbus, Ohio: Merrill.

Drapkin, Martin L. 1996. *Developing Policies and Procedures for Jails: A Step by Step Guide.* Lanham, Maryland: American Correctional Association.

Dupree, David. 1990. *A Guide to Mission Statement Development.* Boulder, Colorado: National Institute of Corrections.

Dupree, David and John Milosovich. 1979. *Policies and Procedures: A Resource Manual.* Boulder, Colorado: National Institute of Corrections.

Houston, James. 1995. *Correctional Management: Functions, Systems, and Skills.* Chicago, Illinois: Nelson-Hall.

Multnomah County Oregon Sheriff's Office http://www.co.multnomah.or.us/sheriff/

New York Police Department. Patrol Services Bureau. http://www.nyc.gov/html/ nypd/html/pct/psb_mission.html

New York Department of Corrections. http://www.docs.state.ny.us/

Page, Stephen B. 2002. *Establishing a System of Policies and Procedures.* Westerville, OH: Process Improvement Publishing.

Page, Stephen B. 2004. *7 Steps to Better Written Policies and Procedures.* Westerville, OH: Process Improvement Publishing.

Pressman, Jeffrey L. and Aaron B. Wildavsky. 1973. *Implementation.* Berkeley: University of California Press.

South Dakota Department of Corrections http://www.state.sd.us/corrections/adult _corrections.htm

Witke, Leonard, ed. 2004. *Planning and Design Guide for Secure Adult and Juvenile Facilities.* Lanham, MD: American Correctional Association.

CHAPTER 6: PLANNING AND THE POLICY PROCESS

Certo, Samuel C. 1985. *Principles of Modern Management,* 3d ed. Dubuque, Iowa: William C. Brown.

David, Fred R. 1986. *Fundamentals of Strategic Management.* Columbus, Ohio: Merrill.

Gibbons, Don C., Joseph L. Thimm, Florence Yospe, and Gerald F. Blake, Jr. 1977. *Criminal Justice Planning.* Englewood Cliffs, New Jersey: Prentice-Hall.

Houston, James. 1995. *Correctional Management: Functions, Skills, and Systems.* Chicago, Illinois: Nelson-Hall.

Hudzik, John K. and Gary W. Cordner. 1983. *Planning in Criminal Justice Organizations and Systems.* New York: Macmillan.

Kast, Freemont and James E. Rosenzweig. 1977. *Organizations and Management: A System and Contingency Approach,* 3d ed. New York: McGraw-Hill.

Knox, George W., Edward D. Tromanhauser, Thomas F. McCurrie, John A. Laskey, James Houston, Bradley L. Martin, and Curtis Robinson. 1996. Preliminary Results of the 1995 Adult Corrections Survey. *Journal of Gang Research* 13(2): 27–63.

Mintzberg, Henry. 1994. *The Rise and Fall of Strategic Planning.* New York: Free Press.

More, Harry W. Jr. and Michael E. O'Neill. 1984. *Contemporary Criminal Justice Planning.* Springfield, Illinois: Charles C. Thomas.

Nanus, Burt. "A General Model for a Criminal Justice Planning Process." *Journal of Criminal Justice* 2(4) (1974): 345–56.

Robbins, Stephen P. 1987. *Organizational Theory: Structure, Design and Application,* 2d ed. Englewood Cliffs, New Jersey: Prentice-Hall.

Stonich, Paul J, 1975. Formal Planning Pitfalls and How to Avoid Them. *Management Review* 64 (Jan., July).

Swanson, Charles R., Leonard Territo, and Robert W. Taylor. 1993. *Police Adminis-tration: Structures, Processes, and Behavior,* 3d ed. New York: Macmillan.

Worthy, James C. "Organizational Structure and Employee Morale," *American Soci-ological Review* (April 1950): 169–79.

CHAPTER 7: TOOLS FOR THE CRIMINAL
JUSTICE POLICY ANALYST

Archambeault, William. 1987. Emerging Issues in the Use of Microcomputers as Management Tools in Criminal Justice Administration. In Joseph Waldron, Betty Archambeault, William Archambeault, Louis Carsone, James Conser, and Carol Sutton, eds. *Microcomputers in Criminal Justice: Current Issues and Applications.* Cincinnati, Ohio: Anderson.

Blalock, Hubert M., Jr. 1979. *Social Statistics,* 2d ed. New York: McGraw-Hill.

Brewer, Garry D. and Peter deLeon. 1983. *The Foundations of Policy Analysis.* Pa-cific Grove, California: Brooks/Cole.

Certo, Samuel. 1985. *Principles of Modern Management: Functions and Systems,* 3d ed. Dubuque, Iowa: Wm. C. Brown.

David, Fred R. 1986. *Fundamentals of Strategic Management.* Columbus, Ohio: Merrill.

Gibbons, Don C., Joseph L. Thimm, Florence Yospe, Gerald F. Blake, Jr. 1977. *Crim-inal Justice Planning.* Englewood Cliffs, New Jersey: Prentice-Hall.

Hirschhorn, Larry. 1982. Scenario Writing: A Developmental Approach. In Richard D. Bingham and Marcus E. Ethridge, *eds.,.Reaching Decisions in Public Policy and Administration.* New York: Longman.

Houston, James. 1995. *Correctional Management: Functions, Skills, and Systems.* Chicago, Illinois: Nelson-Hall.

Hudzik, John K. and Gary W. Cordner. 1983. *Planning in Criminal Justice Organi-zations and Systems.* New York: Macmillan.

Jones, Charles O. 1984. *An Introduction to the Study of Public Policy,* 3d ed. Pacific Grove, California: Brooks/Cole.

Lasswell, Harold D. 1959. "The Social Setting of Creativity." In *Creativity and Its Cultivation,* Harold H. Anderson, ed. New York: Harper and Row.

McEwen, L. Thomas. 1990. *Use of Microcomputers in Criminal Justice Agencies* Washington, DC: Bureau of Justice Assistance.

Schwartz, Peter. 1991. *The Art of the Long View: Planning for the Future in an Un-certain World.* New York: Doubleday.

CHAPTER 8: IMPROVING CRIME POLICY
IN THEORY AND PRACTICE

Anderson, James E. 1994. *Public Policymaking: An Introduction,* 2d ed. Boston, Massachusetts: Houghton Mifflin.

Bonser, Charles E, Eugene B. McGregor, and Clinton V. Oster. 1996. *Policy Choices and Public Action.* Upper Saddle River, New Jersey: Prentice-Hall.

Bums, James M., J. W. Peltason, Thomas Cronin, and David B. Magleby. 1996. *State and Local Politics: Government by the People.* Upper Saddle River, New Jersey: Prentice-Hall.

Dye, Thomas. 1994. *Politics in States and Communities,* 8th ed. Upper Saddle River, New Jersey: Prentice-Hall.

Gibbons, Don C. 1963. Who Knows What about Correction? *Crime and Delinquency* 9 (April): 137–44.

Gibbons, Don C. 1992. *Society, Crime, and Criminal Behavior,* 6th ed. Englewood Cliffs, New Jersey: Prentice-Hall.

Gibbons, Don C., Joseph L. Thimm, Florence Yospe, and Gerald F. Blake. 1977. *Criminal Justice Planning.* Englewood Cliffs, New Jersey: Prentice-Hall.

Gibbs, Jack P. 1968. Crime, Punishment, and Deterrence. *Southwestern Social Science Quarterly* 28 (March): 515–30.

Goodman, Leonard H., Trudy Miller, and Paul De Forrest. 1966. *A Study of the Deterrent Value of Crime Prevention Measures as Perceived by Criminal Offenders.* Washington, DC: Bureau of Social Research.

Houston, James. 1995. *Correctional Management: Functions, Skills, and Systems.* Chicago, Illinois: Nelson-Hall.

Hudzik, John K. and Gary W. Cordner. 1983. *Planning in Criminal Justice Organizations and Systems.* New York: Macmillan.

Jacobs, James. 1977. *Statesville: The Penitentiary in Mass Society.* Chicago, Illinois: University of Chicago Press.

Kast, Freemont and James E. Rosenzweig. 1977. *Organizations and Management: A System and Contingency Approach,* 3d ed. New York: McGraw-Hill.

Knox, George W., Edward D. Tromanhauser, Thomas F. McCurrie, John A. Laskey, James Houston, Bradley L. Martin, and Curtis Robinson. 1996. Preliminary Results of the 1995 Adult Corrections Survey. *Journal of Gang Research* 13(2): 27–63.

Mintzberg, Henry. 1994. *The Rise and Fall of Strategic Planning.* New York: Free Press.

More, Harry W. Jr. and Michael E. O'Neill. 1984. *Contemporary Criminal Justice Planning.* Springfield, Illinois: Charles C. Thomas.

Nanus, Burt. 1974. A General Model for a Criminal Justice Planning Process. *Journal of Criminal Justice 2(4).*

Opheim, Cynthia and Susan B. Day. 1995. *State and Local Politics: The Individual and the Governments,* 2d ed. Reading, Pennsylvania: Addison-Wesley.

Robbins, Stephen P. 1987. *Organizational Theory: Structure, Design and Application,* 2d ed. Englewood Cliffs, New Jersey: Prentice-Hall.

Stone, Clarence N., Robert K. Whelan, and William J. Murin. 1986. *Urban Policy and Politics in a Bureaucratic Age,* 2d ed. Upper Saddle River, New Jersey: Prentice-Hall.

Stonich, Paul J, 1975. Formal Planning Pitfalls and How to Avoid Them. *Management Review* 64 (Jan., July).

Swanson, Charles R., Leonard Territo, and Robert W. Taylor. 1993. *Police Administration: Structures, Processes, and Behavior,* 3d ed. New York: Macmillan.

Susser, Bernard. 1996. *Approaches to the Study of Politics.* New York: Macmillan.
Tittle, Charles R. 1969. Crime Rates and Legal Sanctions. *Social Problems* 16 (Spring): 409–23.
Wilson, James Q. and Joan Petersilia, eds. 1995. *Crime.* San Francisco, California: ICS Press.

SUPREME COURT CASES REFERENCED

Bakke v. California Board of Regents, 1978
Griggs v. Duke Power, 1971
Hamdi et al v Rumsfeld, 2004
Mapp v. Ohio, 1961
Meritor v. Vinson, 1987
Powell v. Alabama, 1932
U.S. Steel v. Weber, 1979

Subject Index